Praise for *Straight Talk for Men About Marriage*...

"I was groping—there had to be more to my marriage, my life, than this! *Straight Talk for Men About Marriage* is whittled-down truth, eloquently spoken. It is not a quick-fix, but a concise road map, showing what's possible and how to get there. It has helped me rediscover my strength, focus and courage. I heartily encourage any married man to read this book and begin this vital journey."

John Brady, Attorney

"Finally, the book about love...written for guys who'd rather watch the game. Marty Friedman offers straight talk and great advice for men who want to have great marriages. When it comes to understanding women, Marty's the man."

Michael Levin, Author, *Stone Cold Sober*

"I recommend Marty Friedman's *Straight Talk for Men About Marriage* without reservation to anyone who wants to learn about communication, relationships and marriage, and who wants to turn his or her problems into breakthroughs."

Michael Ray, Professor Emeritus, Stanford University; Author, *Creativity in Business* and *The Path of the Everyday Hero: The New Paradigm in Business*

"Here's a revolutionary thought for guys who aren't happy at home: What if no one's really at fault in your marriage, it's just that the damn marriage didn't come with instructions—or at least instructions that made any sense to us guys. When it comes to getting solid information about what men can do to get the marriage they want—and keep their wife happy, too—Marty Friedman wrote the book. In fact, this is it!"

Laren Bright, Author, *Laughter: The Best Meditation*

Real Men Don't Read Books on Relationships
They'll Read This One!

Why? Because this one doesn't pull any punches. It doesn't tiptoe around the issues with nice-sounding psycho-talk; it addresses the issues head-on.

What do men want in marriage?

- More sex
- Less criticism

At least those are near the top of the list.

But this isn't a macho, pound-your-chest kind of a book. It deals with the issues of marriage and relationships with intelligence, strength and sensitivity, yet it shows men how to be fully masculine in their marriages.

Marty Friedman gets to the heart of the matter: Guys want good marriages and relationships, just like women do. Really. It's just that their approach is different. And that's the genius of this book; it looks at marriage in ways men and women can relate to and DO something about.

One more thing: There's a section in here for women that gives you an insight into how men think. It's sort of like peeking through the keyhole into the boys' locker room. You might be surprised at what you see and hear. However, you will begin to understand what it all means and how you can use it to make things better between you and your guy.

So, why are we talking about guys as "them" instead of guys as "us" here? Because most men probably aren't browsing in the relationship section. (And those of you men who are, boy have you picked up the right book to help you understand and make your marriage better.) So, if you're a wife or sweetheart who would like an enhanced marriage or relationship, getting this book into your man's hands is up to you.

Straight Talk for MEN About MARRIAGE stands on a bedrock of practical experience. It's written by a man whose 20-year marriage started to crumble and who had the guts and the will to look at it. What he learned has revolutionized his marriage and his life. It can do the same for yours.

Marty Friedman has transferred a successful

25-year career of speaking and consulting in the corporate world into a rewarding career consulting and speaking to men and women on revitalizing their marriages. His career transformation took place when his wife pointed out that their marriage was, for all intents and purposes, over. How he responded to the 2x4 between the eyes created the basis for his new life and career. Prospering in his marriage of over 20 years, Marty is one happy guy. He lives with his wife and children in Northern California.

STRAIGHT TALK FOR
MEN
ABOUT
MARRIAGE

STRAIGHT TALK FOR
MEN
ABOUT
MARRIAGE

What Men Need to Know About Marriage
(And What Women Need to Know About Men)

MARTIN G. FRIEDMAN

LITTLE MOOSE PRESS
Beverly Hills, CA

Straight Talk for MEN About MARRIAGE:
What Men Need to Know About Marriage
(And What Women Need to Know About Men)
Copyright © 2005 Martin G. Friedman

Published by Little Moose Press
269 S. Beverly Drive, #1065
Beverly Hills, CA 90212
www.littlemoosepress.com

Library of Congress Cataloging-in-Publication
Friedman, Martin G., 1948-
Straight talk for men about marriage / Martin G. Friedman.-- 1st ed.
    p. cm.
ISBN 0-9720227-5-9 (alk. paper)
  1. Husbands--United States--Life skills guides. 2. Marriage--United States.
  3. Man-woman relationships--United States. I. Title.
      HQ756.F747 2005
      306.872--dc22
          2004021701

Printed and bound in the United States of America (Acid-free paper)
Cover and book design by Patricia Bacall
Author photo by Bob Hankins
Cover illustration by Veer Images

To the woman who walks with me,
and to the one who lights the way.

ACKNOWLEDGMENTS

A warm thank you to: Michael Butler and B.B. Borowitz for early encouragement and enthusiastic support of my mission; Chris Forsyth for useful help in editing an early version of my manuscript; Michael Levin for kind, incisive and knowledgeable editing; Laren Bright for fun and terrific copy; Ron Kenner for expert copyediting; Patricia Bacall for creative design; Brookes Nohlgren for proofreading and production coordination; and especially Ellen Reid, who lovingly and firmly shepherded me from manuscript to book and well beyond.

CONTENTS

CONTENTS

CONTENTS

CHAPTER ONE

The Challenge of Marriage

YOU, ME AND MARRIAGE

Let's talk, married man to married man.

As we begin, I'd like to tell you a little bit about me and how I came to advise men on marriage.

The first thing you should understand about me is that every word in this book comes from my own experience as a married man. I'm not going to advise you on anything I haven't lived through myself. In my opinion, a man becomes an "expert" on marriage only by personally overcoming its challenges. Anybody who tries to teach others how to be married without having done it himself is a fraud. So, I offer you this book as the fruit of my own struggles in marriage. And you may be surprised when I tell you that my struggles continue. My marriage has always been tempestuous, and I expect the same in the future. So, please don't put me on a pedestal as the "successfully" married guy who's always blissfully happy with his marriage.

Let me tell you more about how I came to know what I know. A few years ago, I never dreamed I would write a book about marriage. During my twenty-two-year marriage my wife and I have raised three children, weathered our share of challenges and managed to keep our family together. But I certainly did not consider myself an "expert" on the subject of marriage.

I have worked as a management consultant for more than twenty-five years, teaching communication skills and management-employee relations to clients worldwide. I've also been practicing Siddha Yoga Meditation for nearly thirty years. Although these experiences have helped me to develop good communication skills and to work well with people, I am neither a trained therapist nor counselor—nor do I want to be! I'm a man who has gone through a lot to become a happier (married) person.

My Wake-Up Call

In recent years, my wife became very excited about her new Ph.D. program in Transpersonal Psychology. She had many new friends and much excitement in her life. My life, on the other hand, had settled into a routine—I'd go to work, come home, have dinner, hang out a little and go to bed early. The next day, I would get up and start it all over again. The routine didn't seem bad; it was simply the way things were and I had grudgingly accepted it. Much later, it occurred to me that I was following my father's example for how to be a husband and father: sacrifice, give your all to your family—and suffer; silently, if possible.

Everything suddenly changed one evening when my wife and I were on a short vacation in Napa Valley in California's wine country. In the midst of a contentious, upsetting conversation it became obvious we had grown so far apart that we were in imminent danger of splitting up. In fact, it was clear that, emotionally, she had already left me.

What happened in the next couple of days changed my life. Through two days and nights of talking, crying, listening and silent periods of reflection and prayer, I saw things clearly for the first time. I saw, in an incredibly plain and lucid way, what marriage could be. I saw the potential for mutual growth and support; how marriage could be "holy" in its own way if both partners could love and respect the other fully, yet with each remaining completely responsible for one's own growth. To this day, I don't know where that "vision" came from, but it was as clear as anything I've seen. I saw a way to create a new marriage for us, and perceived how honesty, commitment and vulnerability could be part of our foundation.

I also realized that my life had become stale and that I had stopped caring. I was sleepwalking through life. I had stopped growing and had ceased to be an interesting partner to my wife. It was painful, but I woke up to how little passion and love I had in my life, despite realizing how much my wife meant to me. For the first time, I committed to do the necessary work to change for the better.

I had spent years, off and on, going to personal counseling sessions with a wonderful counselor. I always considered myself an active and willing participant in those sessions, but I guess I wasn't ready to face some of the "big" issues I needed to face. This time I was determined to return to individual counseling with a new commitment, and I found the experience completely different. I was enthusiastic about the process and passionately committed to uncovering whatever was blocking me from my own "truth"—that is, my own enjoyment and love for life.

I began the inner work to make my marriage the prime focus and to pursue my vision for my wife and me as equal partners in our marriage. I discovered that I wanted more from all aspects of my life, and that I was settling for a lot less and being a "martyr" in the process—just as my father had done. I soon negotiated my way out of a high-paying, high-pressure job that had dulled my senses and into a severance that allowed me some time off.

During my time off, I continued to do my "inner work." I experimented with a new approach to life. I learned to loosen up and enjoy dancing, which I'd never been able to do. I learned to cook a little, to enjoy gardening and to just cherish being alone. I also continued counseling and working to strengthen our marriage. My wife went through a number of life changes too, and she looked at a number of painful things about her own life. Gradually it dawned on me that

I was becoming happier, and that I finally had a passion for a new career that was my true "calling"—to share my new understanding of marriage with others. I did a great deal of research on the history of marriage and I read a good bit of the conventional wisdom, too.

I started a business, *Men in Marriage*. I began to help men through seminars about marriage and relationships, and to consult with individual clients. I also began to talk to women about how men function in relationships. Again, everything I relate here to others is something I've personally experienced or learned and applied. I am not trusting in a theory or in other people's ideas.

What about my marriage today? We still have conflicts and periods of highs and lows—that's married life. But it continues to be a rich vein of insights that fuels growth in my life. My wife and I have drawn closer and developed a much deeper commitment. I feel more love and excitement in my life today than ever before and we are much, much closer.

When I tell you that I understand the troubles men have in their marriages, I hope you will believe me that I can relate to your marriage, that I'm in the trenches with you. This is an unusual book; it is written for men, but not merely from a "therapeutic" viewpoint. I hope you will value what I tell you, because I know it works. I'm giving you sound advice, right from the heart.

I'm going to take a wild guess here that you are like most married men. You want your marriage to be easy, to be set, and not have to worry about it. You want your wife to be fun and to accept you for what you are. You want good sex and you want your home to be a place of refuge. And you don't want to be forced into putting a whole lot of energy into "fixing" yourself or your marriage. You may think you are the only one with a difficult marriage, that other guys surely must have it easier. Very few of them do. The only reason you don't know this is that men don't talk about these things to each other. Around other men, we like to act as though everything's fine. Like most men, there may be a large gap between where your marriage is and where you wish it would be.

You've undoubtedly already put a lot of your energy, time and heart into your marriage. You may be frustrated or even in despair about the course of your marriage. However, whatever its condition, your marriage has potential; marriage is *the* element of your life that can lift you to experience love, change you for the better and provide comfort and support. Some part of you knew that when you got into it. But did you know how hard it would be?

Marriage is challenging. You question whether it's possible to have passion, companionship, good sex and comfort with just one woman for the rest of your life. And you wonder whether you can withstand your wife's emotional ups and downs—she makes you crazy sometimes! Maybe you even question whether you are cut out for monogamy, much less for the married lifestyle. There are plenty of beautiful and available women out there, and the worse your marriage seems the more you look at them.

Children don't turn out to be the answer to a difficult marriage, either. Studies show the hardest time to be married is when you have school-age children. On the other hand, as Franklin P. Jones said, "The most difficult year of marriage is the one you're in." With all the chaos, stimulation and temptations of modern life, divorce may begin to seem like a good option. But there are alternatives. This book is designed to give you power—the power to have a better marriage and a better life with your wife.

We men feel powerless around the subject of "relationships." In fact, we don't even want to talk about relationships. We can be focused and passionate about work, politics, gadgets, sports, sex (not necessarily in that order) or many other things, but not about "the relationship." By contrast, women love to dissect relationships, contemplate them, reflect on them, despair about them and generally obsess about them. But for men, the most dreaded thing a wife can say is, "Sit down; I want to talk about our relationship!"

Wife: "We need to talk about our relationship…"

Husband: "Do we have to do it now?"

Wife: "Yes."

Husband: "OK, but there's a game starting soon that I want to see."

Wife: "Fine. So, what do you think about our relationship?"

Husband: "What?"

Wife: "What do you think is going on with our relationship? We see each other every day; you must have some opinion about it. How are we doing?"

Husband: (Clueless about what to say; what if he says the wrong thing?!) "It's going OK, I guess…"

Wife: "Are you kidding? Don't you see the trouble we're in? Don't you see that our relationship right now is sick?"

Husband: "Sick? What are you talking about? You're making way too big a deal out of this. What do you want out of me? Do you just sit around and look for ways to criticize me?"

(At this point, the wife begins to enumerate the various ways the relationship is "sick" and why the husband's behavior is the root of many, if not all, of their relationship problems. The husband sits there in a daze, knowing he will be unable to watch the game until he takes his punishment.)

Women do seem to have better built-in relationship skills—they speak and understand the language while we can't even find the dictionary! But that's OK. You will learn in this book how to have a relationship that works for you—without having to compete with your wife on her home turf of relationship discussions. You'll learn some new ideas and beliefs about marriage and men and women that should make a big difference in your life and marriage. Now, let's continue to dive into the topic of marriage—past, present and future.

MEN SUFFER IN MARRIAGE—
BUT DON'T WANT TO TALK ABOUT IT

*"Marriage can be compared to a cage: The birds outside are
frantic to get in and those inside frantic to get out."*
—Montaigne, 1588

Ah, marriage…heaven and hell and everything in between. I have
done an informal survey of the men in my seminars and audiences, as
well as among men I met elsewhere. When I ask men for their top two
complaints about their wife or long-term lover, I'm amazed at the
degree of agreement in their responses. Way over ninety percent say
roughly the same thing: "Not enough sex, and too much criticism."
A great many men are frustrated by the lack or quality of sex and
shamed by the constant criticism by their wives. We will deal at
some length later with each of these. But the strange thing is that
most men are suffering in their marriages to a large degree, yet won't,
or can't, do anything about it or even talk about their suffering. For
some reason, men will soldier on in pain and not change anything
about their marriages unless their wives tell them to.

As I look around at married men I know, they generally fall into
two camps. One group is composed of men who actively dislike their
marriages. These men are either completely alienated from their
wives or they burn with resentment. Men in the other group are generally OK with their marriages, yet they are suffering and flailing a
bit because they want more out of it but can't figure out how to manage this. I want to tell you how you can have a marriage that works
for you, regardless of where you fit. But, first we will have to take
apart the way you view marriage and your commitment to it.

Everyone who's dissatisfied thinks his marriage is the only one
that's troubled. Nobody else's wife, he thinks, could be so emotional… so changeable… so demanding… so hard to satisfy.
Everyone else must have a good marriage, because yours has holes

7

in it! But is there such a thing as a "good" marriage? Every marriage has a range of experiences built into it, good and bad. Marriage is like life itself—joyful, scary, maddening and challenging. It includes inevitable suffering, like all human existence, yet contains the potential for the greatest love and satisfaction. Marriage is masculine and feminine energy combined to create a unified whole. Every time you think it's set, your marriage changes. It's as slippery as mercury; how can you ever hold on?

The book you are reading is written to change and empower your values and beliefs about marriage. The way you experience marriage is largely determined by the beliefs and values you hold about it. In countries where arranged marriages still flourish, men and women have very different views than people in the West. People in those countries don't expect to find romantic love and personal fulfillment from marriage—to them, marriage is a matter of companionship, survival, division of labor and child rearing. For Westerners raised on images of romance and "happily ever after," marriage is generally believed to hold the key to happiness. If it doesn't pay off that way, trouble ensues. And the situation is more difficult for men today than ever before. Through hundreds of thousands of years of evolution, we have evolved with the physiology and mindset to act as warriors, to be men of action and accomplishment. But in 21st-century marriages we often feel powerless, befuddled and frustrated. How did we get to this difficult place? There are many answers, but let's start with a look back.

WHERE HAVE WE BEEN AND WHERE ARE WE GOING?

Marriage is difficult today in a way that it never was before. For thousands of years men and women got married to produce children, create financial security and have companionship throughout life. A man took care of his wife and children by providing financial and/or physical security. A wife took care of her husband and children and was in charge of the house. In this stable arrangement, husbands and wives alike usually found their expectations met. If not, the couple usually stayed together anyway. Marriage roles were so clear-cut and widely accepted for thousands of years that they required no discussion—even though they placed both men and women into often painful, constricting boxes.

Part of the reason marriages used to be so stable was that women lacked the economic power and confidence to live comfortably on their own. Forty years ago, divorce laws made the dissolution of marriage more difficult than it is today. And our social institutions and popular media proclaimed the pleasure and supremacy of a stable, long-lasting family unit. (Think "Leave It to Beaver" and "Father Knows Best" on television in the '50s.) Men stayed in marriages because they were *supposed* to. Women stayed in marriages because they *had* to. Divorces were relatively rare.

We men have had it really good until very recently. In nearly every recorded culture throughout history, men have enjoyed extensive marital power through tradition, religious doctrines, money and law. For at least four or five thousand years, men could easily fulfill the role of a husband, yet still attend to matters "outside the house"—do our work, hang out with other men and, at times, even have sex with other women. For most of recorded history, men never expected to have romantic love through their marriages, and many men were known to get their sexual satisfaction and intimacy through visits to a prostitute or courtesan. As long as we provided for our families, the law and the institutions of society were on our side.

The old equation for marriage was simple: *The husband provides security, and the wife takes care of the husband, children and household.*

Until very recently, marriage primarily enabled procreation, survival, security and family. Husbands and fathers were often remote, lofty, powerful figures scarcely involved in the emotional life of their marriages and families. Although it sometimes happened during the course of the marriage, men were not expected to enter into an intimate, interpersonal relationship with their wives. The husband, as well as being the provider, was expected to be an upstanding and relatively virtuous member of society. But in practically every culture in the Western world, for many centuries—and continuing still in many parts of the world—one's wife was considered by society and law to be little more than property. Though suffocating in many respects, such an arrangement provided a stable marriage and family environment, and met the simple needs of most husbands and wives.

Toward the end of the 19th century, the way people looked at marriage began to change. The primary reason was that people began to believe that romantic love was the *necessary prerequisite* for marriage. Books, popular songs and, later, movies sent out the message that romantic love is wonderful and that every married person deserves to have romance with his or her marriage partner. Men were told to pick a woman for love and, significantly, took an oath to be responsible for maintaining love and passion throughout marriage.

Along with the rise of romantic love, man's supremacy was weakened. Women began to gain increased legal rights in property and divorce settlements, and, of course, they began to enter the workplace in unprecedented numbers during the first part of the 20th century, especially during World War II. Gradually, men's secure place in the home was threatened and the clear, traditional role of "husband" became obscured in the murky waters of social change.

By the 1950s and 1960s, recently married men may not have realized as much but they were standing on shaky ground. They were still trying to hold on to a 19th-century conception of marriage in a new, postwar framework. Large numbers of men were locked into a soulless job; yet at home were still expected to be strong, confident and manly while providing everything for their families without complaining.

When I meet men from the World War II generation, men in their 70s and above, I am struck by how differently they think about their marriages. The men of the Depression and World War II knew what to expect from their marriages: companionship, loyalty, sex and stability—but not necessarily much else. When I listen to many of them talk about their fifty- or sixty-year marriages, they don't talk much about "fulfillment" or "intimacy" or "support." They talk mostly about companionship and friendship, and about a simple division of labor in the home.

In the World War II generation, a man expected to stay married and provide for his family, regardless of the situation, and he expected his wife to take care of the home and of them. And like countless generations before, the marriage lasted and the man "wore the pants" in the house, at least ostensibly. The World War II generation was surely the last purely patriarchal one in the United States.

In many ways, compared to current standards, marriage up to 1964 may have been quite unfulfilling to both husband and wife; but the role of each in marriage seemed clear. Yet an earthquake was beginning to rumble beneath the shaky, ancient edifice called marriage. The changes that began in Western society in the 1960s, such as feminism, sexual freedom and political instability, combined with the decreased power of governmental, religious and educational institutions to weaken marriage and make divorce a more acceptable and common option.

When the upheaval of the '60s and '70s threw marriage roles into question, men felt pressured to change. The problem then, as well as now, is that men lacked a clear picture of how to create a long-term relationship or marriage in this new world. How can the old marriage model thrive amid modern circumstances such as an "empowered" wife, relaxed divorce laws, women with careers and often diametrically different sexual expectations?

Men desperately need a new understanding of the husband's role, and they need some new skills to create a workable, thriving marriage. In an effort to please women, many men have tried to become "New Age" and more "feminized" and have fallen into a quagmire of weakness. Others have held on to the antiquated view of the strong, silent, macho husband, watching their marriages crumble as their wives demanded more even though they couldn't, or wouldn't, change.

I have written this book convinced that marriage is important to men, and that any man can learn what it takes to make marriage more fulfilling. Men are put together differently; we usually have to learn relationship skills that most women naturally possess. Women may criticize us as "competitive," "closed-off," "inexpressive" and "unfeeling." You've probably heard some of these criticisms leveled at men. One thing I don't do in this book is "male bashing." There is too much of that in our culture already. (Just watch television commercials and sitcoms to learn about how dumb and useless men are supposed to be.) Contrary to what you hear, males bring valuable things to a marriage. One of the most important is the power to take action. Strangely, men underutilize this power in their marriages.

Let's look a little deeper at how you can apply your natural power of action to your marriage.

MEN ARE CUT OUT TO TAKE ACTION
(BUT MOST MEN JUST *REACT* TO THEIR WIVES
AND THEIR MARRIAGES)

It's amazing that so many married men are unhappy with their marriages and feel stuck and resentful yet do very little to change things. We men usually don't act at all on our marriages until our wives make it impossible to avoid the issues any longer. After they rattle our cages, we may act—grudgingly. Our wives drag us to counseling. We trudge into "relationship workshops," or we try to sit still for books, tapes, videos or endless "relationship talks," all the while wishing we were somewhere else. Worse still, when we do listen, we are told that we are the problem! No wonder we avoid looking at our relationships or marriages.

Men are naturally inclined to act, to build tangible and intangible structures and to solve problems—but when it comes to our marriages, we'd rather ignore what's going on around us and turn on the television. Time after time I talk to women who come to my seminars and speeches and tell me that their husbands are ignoring them and their children. One woman told me that her husband plays four or five hours of golf each day, ignoring his wife and children; another said her husband retreats to his office and stares at a computer screen all night, every night. You and I know that many times when we find something to do it's to build our businesses or careers. But many other times it's because our wives are so critical and unappreciative of what we do that we'd just as soon not be home. But what price are we paying? At my seminars for men I often see the "walking wounded"—men who are walking though life without emotion or interest. They have become estranged from their wives and from their own energy and interest in life. When I ask them how their marriages are, invariably they tell me that their wives have just about given up on them, and that they have given up on their own marriages. Were they aware of their marriage problems? No! Not until their wives began to shake the bars of their cages through threats to leave them.

Let's make this personal: your inaction, or focus on other things at the exclusion of your marriage, is only driving your wife farther away and making you unhappy. What recourse do you have? Take the natural power of action inherent in men and pour it into your marriage to build it up and make it better. Overcome your fear of change and of dealing with your own feelings. Your fear is in the way of your potential for aliveness and power. Start now. Resolve to deal with your internal issues and get your power back—all in the context of your marriage.

Besides the simple power of action, men have much more generally unacknowledged natural talent that can be useful in a relationship. Men can define a problem and solve it with laser focus. We have the power to dream and put our dreams into concrete action, and to make powerful commitments and stick to them. We are able to keep our distance from the daily swirl of feelings, because our biology allows us to focus intensely on our "prey"—whatever it may be. Men have the power to stand for something great and to fight for it with resolve and unswerving power. Add to these qualities the primitive male instinct to protect and care for our wives and families—whatever the cost to ourselves. If you want your marriage to work for you, you'll need to put all of these male strengths to work in your marriage and add some new ones that you may think of as "feminine"—but aren't. The results will be overwhelmingly positive.

Any man who isn't confused and intimidated when he tries to determine the proper role for a husband at the beginning of the 21st century just isn't paying attention. Acknowledge any of your fears and feelings of powerlessness or alienation in your marriage and you'll find you are not alone. What you feel is real, and it's understandable. Giving up isn't the answer. The answer is to take an active role in the marriage and to get your power back.

There are ways to make it work. But you will have to put your energy and skills into some things that may be new to you. It's worth it—you don't want to be one of those sad, forlorn men we all know: miserable, bruised guys who have stubbornly clung to their macho, closed-off ways only to lose their wives and families through painful divorces.

The men who will feel powerful in their marriages in the 21st century will be those who give up the old equation of marriage and discover the power inside themselves, rather than in their traditional role as a husband and father. You can start this process by looking honestly, relentlessly and compassionately at yourself and your marriage. The power you need to make your marriage succeed already resides within.

A WORD ABOUT WOMEN AND POWER

Over the same years that women obtained more legal, political and social rights, romantic love blossomed in the popular imagination. These two parallel trends didn't occur by accident. It seems very likely that the rise of women's rights caused the ascension of romantic love. Once women possessed more power and significance in their own right, they became more interesting to themselves—and to men. From the point of view of sexual and romantic tension, women's power was, and is, a good thing. On the other hand, women may also become more threatening as they seem to need us less and are less available for mothering and nurturing.

Women are learning how to use their new power in the workplace, at home and in society at large. As this process continues, they will be testing the bounds of what it means to be female and more unwilling to play old, traditional female roles. If the purpose of marriage is to learn to love, then you will benefit most if you see your wife as a powerful equal—just like you and worthy of your love.

Powerful women can upset the traditional balance of marriage. When women enter the workplace, they often access their male power to get things done, and they may have a difficult time turning it off when they get home. They may come home tired, wired up and cranky—just like the man after a day at the office. The wife may be unable or unwilling to take up her old nurturing role, and this can be threatening and upsetting to her husband. As a society, we are a long way off from solving these issues. Some women are returning to their homemaker roles. Others are electing to raise their children first before making a career. However it plays out with your own wife, you will find one reliable solution: find your own power and you will feel less threatened by hers.

You will feel diminished by your wife's power only if you are not feeling powerful or not having some of your needs met. If your wife's attention to her own career or other interests is affecting you negatively, tell her, without blaming or criticizing, how you feel and what you need. Get together and figure out a way to budget time and focus to feed your marriage. But be careful not to force your wife to take care of you at her own expense. This attitude will only weaken you and cause her to move farther away.

>Support your wife's ability to become her genuine powerful self. Don't hold her back. Authentic personal power is compatible with love and family life, so long as it is accompanied by genuine communication and cooperation and respect.

As a loving mate, it's your job to help your wife become a more powerful person. If this seems difficult, remember: it's said that power is the ultimate aphrodisiac!

It is possible to have a fulfilling marriage, and it's worth the effort. However, you may need to change the way you have been looking at marriage and its place in your life. Actually, you may well need to alter your understanding about commitment, sex, conflicts, love and the purpose of marriage itself. Helping you make that change is what this guidebook is all about. Here is the bottom line: If you are willing to do the work on yourself, you can tremendously influence the course of your marriage. If you aren't, you may as well prepare yourself to face a difficult or failed marriage.

Your marriage is a huge part of your life, and it can offer much happiness and growth. If your marriage is generally OK, the principles in this book will help you make it better. If you are suffering in your marriage, this book will help you gain a measure of confidence and build a road map to get your marriage on track. These ideas are offered to inspire and guide you to create a marriage that brings you love—a feeling of aliveness and power.

I do not have all the answers. I know that the right answers for you will ultimately come from you. I offer this book as a guide to those men who sincerely want to reach for a life of aliveness, power and love. I hope it provides you with some guideposts on your journey and I truly wish you well in your exploration. Now let's get specific about what to do so you can begin to create the kind of marriage you want. Read on to learn the three important steps you must take.

CHAPTER TWO

Step One: Create a Vision for Your Marriage and Lead the Way

REACH FOR A POWERFUL MARRIAGE

A satisfying marriage can help you to be the person you always knew you could be—loving, centered and alive. You may not believe it, but you will only have a truly full and satisfying life if your marriage is satisfying as well.

Many men feel powerful and alive in their work, yet settle for a married life that is unexciting and stale. They fool themselves, thinking that if they just focus on their work or children, they can ignore a difficult marriage. A man like this is like a soldier with a gaping chest wound who goes into battle saying, "Oh, I'm fine, no problem, guys!" Meanwhile, he staggers around, covered in blood, and picks up his gun to fight. A man whose marriage isn't working is one of the "walking wounded," regardless of what he says about how much of a success he is in his working life.

You may lurch around with a bullet in your gut, fixed smile in place, until either your wife threatens to leave you or you find other women for the excitement, sex and love you originally wanted from your wife. Or, you will continue lurching on until your jagged marriage creates gaping wounds that manifest problems in your physical body, your relationships or your work.

Men want to be powerful and strong. We all have the capacity to throw ourselves into something wholeheartedly, to give our all. But we tend to give the best part of ourselves to our work, because we feel most at home there. We may display confidence, fire, generosity and wholeness in our careers or vocations. Perhaps this pattern fits you: you pour yourself into your work, but in the most serious, fundamental relationship of your life (your marriage) you are probably less than confident—even baffled—by the course it has taken. Most men gauge how well their marriage is functioning according to whether their wife has yelled at them recently! This attitude weakens our essential, great male power.

I'm sure you did not start out expecting your life to be only "half" great, or to live a "partially" great life. How do you separate a marriage from the rest of your life when it is such a fundamental part of your time on this earth? Are you ready to take a good hard look at your marriage? The first thing we need to address is your commitment.

MAKE A NEW COMMITMENT TO YOUR MARRIAGE

All details aside, it's your ego that prevents you from realizing the real predicament you are in and from actively shining a spotlight on your marriage. Have the courage to put your focus and energy into this essential part of your life. It may be difficult. It may be confusing and painful at times. Ultimately it is your choice: leave your marriage the way it is and muddle through life, or take steps to jump-start your marriage and your life.

The first thing you have to do is to decide that you are fully in your marriage for the long haul—you have to determine that it is worth your time, energy and attention. To build the marriage you want, make a commitment that you will stay and participate in your marriage, *unconditionally*. Take a stand that you won't leave your wife; if she wants to leave, that can be her choice. *But quitting is not an option for you.* Like all men, you will function best when your heart and soul are fully engaged in battle.

Would you have respect for a man at your work who is merely going through the motions, questioning whether he should even be there? Wouldn't you want to shove him out the door? A man who is constantly questioning his marriage is like this. "Is this the right woman for me?" "Should I stand for this?" "Do I really need to put up with this?" A man like this doesn't earn a lot of respect, even though we can be compassionate about his suffering. The same goes for a man who is ignoring his marriage entirely. Both types of men are going to reap what they plant. A man who isn't fully committed to his marriage is a man who is guaranteed to be miserable.

An attorney who attended one of my seminars had gotten extremely distant from his wife. Their marriage had become lifeless and routine. He returned home to his wife the same night, engaged, focused and fully "in" the marriage. To his shock, she indicated that she wanted to have sex with him, which was something they hadn't done for several months! (He accepted.) Why the change in his wife? Simply because he was ready to take a powerful stand for his own marriage—to put all his attention, mind and heart into the enterprise.

I am asking you to take a dangerous step. I am asking you to jump off a cliff and land in the realm of "relationship." If you are like most men, the inner workings of your marriage just aren't that interesting to you. If you had it your way, maybe your marriage would be simple, stable and trouble-free—somewhat like a relationship with one of your male friends, except you'd have the benefit of being with a woman for sex and nurturance. The trouble is no relationship with a woman is going to be that simple and straightforward. Women are more complicated than men and they care more about issues in "the relationship" that you've probably never even considered. And when you jump off that cliff, you are landing on unfamiliar ground. More than that, I'm saying that you have to be absolutely committed to staying there and acting in a powerful, accomplished way. I'm absolutely confident that you can do it.

21

To succeed, you will need to figure out what you want out of your marriage. Just like a business problem, you need to start with the goal in mind and have a plan to get where you want to go. Men work best when they feel in control, when they know where their efforts will take them. Probably most of what you've done in the past has been to react to your marriage, rather than to move purposefully. As strange as it may sound, if you are going to change your marriage so it works for you, you will need to create a vision for your marriage.

YOUR MARRIAGE VISION:
A POWERFUL AND ALIVE MARRIAGE

A vision is an inspirational goal that you feel emotionally motivated to follow and achieve. This ability, to move in a straight line and ignore everything but the goal, is perhaps a man's greatest strength—and his greatest weakness. Innate in men throughout history, this capacity to focus on the battle has proved critical not only for winning battles in war but for winning over competition in work and sports. It has moved men to stupendous feats of courage and daring at all stages of life.

But it has its drawbacks. While women can feel what's wrong in a marriage (and tell us all about it), we may instead focus solely on work, sports, money or politics and leave the "squishy stuff" to our wives. This can easily become a disadvantage in a marriage because, when we do this, we defer responsibility to our wives. No marriage can thrive when only one person takes responsibility for its success.

Use your male strength—the ability to focus, commit and get things done—and turn it to the task of improving your marriage. I'm going to show you how to stand up for the purpose of your marriage and to create your own marriage vision. When you have a clear marriage vision, you'll get your marriage on the right track. Your wife will be more inclined to align with you and respect you more when you are crystal clear about what you want and when you resolve to do what's necessary to reach your goals for *you*, rather than to please *her*.

If, out of fear, inertia or inexperience, you have stopped putting your life energy into your marriage, don't hide out any longer! Your abilities are up to the task and you can harvest the enormous benefits of a rich marriage.

As noted, male testosterone and thousands of years of evolution give men the ability and inclination to be **warriors**. As a man, you have the capacity to be strong, resolute and courageous in your pursuit of a righteous vision. So, stand for something great—the vision of your own marriage as a vehicle for love, growth and true fulfillment. Your marriage will improve and you will feel better about yourself. I call this being the relationship "warrior," the one in the partnership who stands firm in his commitment, vision, strength and purpose. A man like this is a mountain; he can't be moved, he can't be disregarded and he has tremendous power to influence his partner.

If a man is the relationship warrior, what would the woman's role be? Let your wife be the relationship "manager." Women are generally much more proficient at sensing, guiding, prodding and administering the details of a life together. Look at your own marriage: Doesn't your wife understand the subtle dimensions of your marriage better than you? How about the complexities of running your household (laundry, dishes, children, decorating, etc.)? Although the specifics may vary, women are nearly always better at holding multiple details in their consciousness as they manage relationships; it's their natural talent, not yours. Your natural role is to be the keeper of the relationship vision, the one who holds strong in his commitment to a greater good.

What should be the components of your unique marriage vision? The following pages state some of the building blocks you can use as a foundation to create a marriage vision that speaks to both you and your wife.

CREATE AN "H" MARRIAGE—
NOT AN "A" OR AN "I" MARRIAGE

What kind of marriage do you want to create?

Think of a husband and wife as two straight lines. The lines may lean on each other to create the two sides of an "A." If they do, they each become dependent and enmeshed, and stay weak and needy. Each props the other up to prevent falling. "A" marriages presume that each party is somewhat broken and requires intensive care to survive. "A" marriages strengthen the bonds of our egos, creating attachments that might feel good in the short term, but in the long term such marriages become our downfall.

In an "H" marriage, on the other hand, the husband and wife grow independently while staying connected through intimate communication, respect and love. In an "H" marriage, the assumption is that each party grows in a parallel fashion toward more inner strength, in a way unique to each person. In an "H" marriage, you stand for your own growth as well as your wife's. Through strong resolve, mutual goals and similar values, you stay together to support your independent expansion. The connecting line between the two sides of the "H" represents intimate communication and the bond of love. When one side of the "H" grows stronger, it influences the other side to grow stronger, too. This kind of marriage is difficult, but it gets easier as each person grows beyond limited aspects of their personality and becomes a stronger individual. It's a paradox, but you will have the most loving marriage when each of you grows independently as well as together.

Some couples create a "too-wide" H. The vertical lines of the H get so far apart that their marriage becomes business-like, a series of meetings about schedules, kids and finances. They may inhabit the same house, but they become almost strangers to each other. This kind of marriage lacks love and aliveness. It feels dry and empty to the participants. In the past, such marriages were very typical, because the expectations for intimacy and communication in marriage were less and because the demands of economic or physical survival were so great. Today, a "wide H" marriage may end in infidelity or divorce; or, if it survives, will bring only coldness and bitterness to the man and woman involved. When men or women become workaholics, this is the kind of marriage they create because their attention and energy is used up in work and their home life suffers.

On the other hand, some couples create an H whose vertical lines are so close together that they merge to become an "I." This kind of marriage feels smothering and claustrophobic. The partners have little "alone" time. Each submerges his or her individual autonomy and growth in the other person. Each represses individual interests, hobbies or friends. Everything becomes "we" focused; what "we" like, "our" friends, restaurants, travels and activities. "I" marriages breed enmeshment and dependency even more than "A" marriages. It's great to feel close to your wife. But if you get too close your inner spark will be dampened so much that you'll eventually feel desperately lost. After a while, you'll wonder who you are and it will be hard to find your way back. You'll lose the thread. A man in this kind of marriage becomes increasingly emasculated as he merges with his wife. "I" marriages are the kiss of death to your masculine power.

The separation of an "H" marriage doesn't necessarily mean being physically away from your wife. You can learn to be separate from your wife (not merged) even if you are in the same bed with her. Similarly, you can be merged with your wife even if you are miles away. Healthy separation comes from an inner stance, not physical proximity.

STEPS TO HEALTHY SEPARATION

One key to being separate is to take responsibility for your feelings—to notice them, understand them and discover where they come from. Most uncomfortable feelings have a lot to tell you if you listen and stay with them. Feelings don't drop from the sky. They come from unresolved issues that you can uncover and explore.

The reason men don't want to deal with them is that feelings seem to be "in the way" of getting things done or having a good time—and that is true. But pushing emotions away only makes them stronger, and they will keep coming back until we deal with them, usually at the expense of relationships and our joy of life. Besides, your wife will surely notice your feelings and often feel compelled to "manage" them, one way or another. This will drive a wedge between the two of you and increase her anger and resentment.

Another key is to learn to "parent" yourself, rather than expecting your wife to do the job. This means that you can learn to soothe your hurt feelings from childhood or the present, and to be gentle and kind to yourself when you are hurting emotionally, instead of expecting your wife to take care of you.

Nearly every man transfers his feelings for his mother onto his wife, at least sometimes. It's very easy to expect your wife to mother you. A lot of women will comfort and nurture just as mothers do, or "should" have done. A certain amount of this is OK, but if it becomes habitual it will drain you both and inhibit a lively, powerful man-woman relationship.

THE "H" MARRIAGE AND YOUR PERSONAL NEEDS

Your own needs motivate much of your behavior toward your wife; "Let's go to a movie!" (the need for stimulation), or "Come here and give me a hug" (the need for affection) or "I'm hungry" (the need for food). This is understandable. All human beings have needs.

However, some needs are much more subtle and we are unaware of them. For example, maybe you've had a difficult day and when you get home you feel sad or angry about something at work. Perhaps you have an unconscious need for security and comfort. You want your wife to nurture you a little and cook something you really like. Maybe you want sex from her so you can forget the whole damn thing and release your stress.

If you are not conscious of these needs, they will pollute the atmosphere with your wife. They will be between the two of you all night long whether you mention them or not. If you aren't careful, these unacknowledged needs will make you become so needy that you will resent your wife if she doesn't take care of you.

If you practice being separate from your wife, you will see the needs as they come up and you will manage them yourself. Maybe you can "parent" yourself, as described above, and give yourself some of the nurturing you need. Perhaps you can simply ask your wife in a respectful way for what you need, giving her the opportunity to grant your request or decline it. "Honey, I've had a really tough day. Would you come sit with me for a minute and give me a little affection?"

It's important to have a life outside of marriage—interests, friends and external stimulation. It's even more important to do the inner work to become a healthy, separate person so that when you are apart you are fine, and when you are together you can be fully present, available and connected. That's how you go about establishing an "H" marriage.

As we have seen, "A" marriages bring dependency and stagnation. "I" marriages wipe out your individuality and make growth difficult. Healthy "H" marriages create and support powerful, interdependent lives.

The Purpose of Marriage

In my seminars I ask men, "What is the purpose of marriage?" A typical group list looks like this:

- To have children
- Companionship
- Fun activities
- Sex
- Someone to be with when I get lonely
- To merge money and other resources
- Love
- Someone to take care of me when I get old

All of these are perfectly good reasons to be married. Now I'm going to ask you the question I ask men in my seminars: "Is your marriage purpose right now enough to keep you in the game? In fact, are any of these purposes enough to keep you married right now, and in the future?" Children grow up; your companion gets tiresome and you want another one; sex is good sometimes, but you probably don't get it enough or the right way—and even if you do, is it really enough to keep you interested for the rest of your life? Are any of these reasons enough to keep you interested enough to stay married for the rest of your life? Even love, which is unarguably an essential purpose of marriage, may not be enough. This is because the experience of love may come and go—especially if you think you will "get" love from your mate.

The *only* reliable purpose of marriage—the one that will keep you interested and engaged the rest of your life—is to use your marriage as the vehicle for you to learn about yourself, become a better human being and learn to love your wife fully. This is the "H" marriage.

You can probably think of a million excuses why you haven't had the kind of marriage you want. None of them matter now. What's important is that you fully seize the power of creation. Set your mind and heart on the attainment of an "H" marriage—and lead the way.

We've delved a bit into the purpose of marriage. We haven't mentioned what makes marriage so difficult: the clash of egos. So, before we investigate further some of the ingredients of your marriage vision, we'd better look at our old friend the ego and see how it shapes our experience of marriage.

THE ULTIMATE PURPOSE OF MARRIAGE: TO MAKE YOU STRONGER AND REVEAL YOUR TRUE SELF

As we have seen, marriage can provide many things: companionship, sex, parenthood, emotional support and much more. Ultimately, the best purpose of marriage is to help each individual grow in his or her capacity to experience love. This is also the purpose of life and why marriage can be seen as a great life-path. Why then is marriage so difficult? It is the inevitable clash of the two egos that causes friction.

Your ego tends to inhibit what you are truly searching for in life—the experience of completeness and inner strength. What is the ego exactly? It is the sense of separateness and selfishness that each human being has as part of the makeup of his or her personal identity. The ego demands that you put your selfish needs first, very similar to a two-year-old child. The ego also tries to protect itself from things that make it feel insecure, causing us to constantly strive to compete and do all we can to protect ourselves from others.

The ego becomes a problem in a marriage because it is a very selfish tendency. It blocks your ability to experience love because you become so busy trying to get more love and attention from your spouse that you can't focus on anything beyond yourself. The ego is all about "me" and "my needs." And the ego is constantly worried about measuring up and "winning," even when there isn't a competition to be won. Ultimately you will never truly love your wife if you can't feel complete and whole on your own first. And this requires moving past your ego.

Each of us has stored patterns of emotional and mental responses that are revealed during the course of a marriage and that are uniquely linked to our ego. For example, one man I know isolates himself because he is afraid of being dominated. As a consequence, he refuses to compromise and makes unreasonable demands so that he can have his way. You can imagine how resentful this makes his wife.

In my own case, I have gradually discovered my own fears of being abandoned. Because they were unexamined, the fears damaged my marriage—and me. Because of those fears, I had a habit of being emotionally dependent on my wife, in a sense asking her to take care of me in subtle and not-so-subtle ways. If I was sick, I wanted her to be my caretaker and mommy. If I had troubles, I wanted to throw them at her feet. If I was emotionally weak, I wanted her to prop me up. (This sounds suspiciously like an "A" marriage though I would have denied it at the time.) Over time, I saw that my wife was resentful of her role in my drama, and I realized that by relying so much on her I was robbing myself of the chance to get stronger. What a damaging pattern! In recent years, I've worked on this a lot and gotten a better handle on it. Without marriage where would I have learned these important lessons? Without an intimate relationship, what would have shown me these negative tendencies?

Emotional patterns like these are stored deep in our subconscious. Although self-destructive, they usually feel familiar and comfortable. And because they seem so familiar, we cling to them as if they were ours. Unless you are vigilant, your marriage will drown in the waves of your repetitive unconscious patterns, and the patterns will create recurring personality and power struggles between you and your spouse. The sad irony is that almost all of your difficulties with your wife have their roots in the patterns, projections and fears emanating from your own ego.

Let's take one common tendency of the ego: Wanting to have control of every situation. If you want control of your wife, you are doomed to failure. But, if the ego is in charge, you will persist in trying. The result is frustration and anger, and in extreme cases physical and mental abuse. Any attempt to dominate your wife comes from your ego.

At the outset, didn't marriage seem to offer a life of love, peace and completeness? The fact that this promise doesn't pay off is enough to inflame your ego and make you blame, criticize and resent your partner sometimes. However, this built-in frustration inherent in marriage also contains the seed of something fabulous: the situations and challenges you need to help tame the selfish tendencies of your ego and to become more compassionate, caring, loving and strong. Just by being around your wife and paying close attention, you will see the habits, patterns and tendencies that come between the two of you. You can run, but it will only hurt you both—and your destructive ways will be there to meet you when you stop running.

Seen through this lens, marriage is a crucible. If you enter the union with conscious attention and respect, it will help you burn away unnecessary emotional and mental patterns. This process can be painful. Yet, if you consciously participate, it will change your life for the better. And here's a bonus: As your ego gets in your way less and less, you will have fewer conflicts, more sex and less criticism from your wife.

If this approach sounds difficult or harsh, consider the alternative. A bad marriage is a giant grinding wheel smashing all aspects of your life. Are you going to let it grind you down to powder? Or are you going to take charge of the wheel, your marriage and your life?

31

Since we're addressing some difficult topics, let's look at another. The reason that many people get married is to have a feeling of emotional security. People think they'll have someone they can always count on, someone to be there for them no matter what. This is a great picture. However, as the saying goes, "Be careful what you wish for." Please read on and I'll explain what I mean.

MARRIAGE AND EMOTIONAL SECURITY

Frank, age 54, loved his wife, Wanda. He told her and everyone else that Wanda was the key to everything for him. He always said that his life would be over if anything ever happened to her—she was that precious to him. He doted on her—brought her flowers, always offered to do chores around the house or help her cook and wash dishes. Seeking to empathize with her troubles, Frank paid rapt attention when she talked and stuck close by her side, spending every weekend home with his family. Frank depended on her to be his only confidant and support, and eventually let all his male friendships go. In fact, he wouldn't make a decision without her help.

As the years went by, he began to need her to take care of his bad feelings, to tell him what he felt and to give him advice. Any time Frank felt bad he knew that Wanda would make him feel better. Over time, Wanda became weighted down by Frank's overreliance on her. Wanda's health began to deteriorate, and she began to resent Frank's dependence on her. She realized she couldn't be the lifeline for all of his needs anymore because she didn't have enough energy for her own pursuits. Wanda was thinking seriously about leaving him when a routine examination led to the discovery of breast cancer. Within six months she was dead. Frank was devastated—she was his whole life.

After a few months of misery and grief, Frank went through the motions of working but it was clear to everyone that he had given up on life. Within two years, Frank was dead from complications of a bleeding ulcer. But those who knew him knew the truth: Frank died because his wife had left him.

What is the moral of this story? True emotional security can come through the lessons of marriage—but not through dependence on a woman.

Many men are married because they want a woman to take care of them and their feelings. Men like this want their wives to be the doorway to their own feminine energy—the world of feelings, intuition and nurturance. This is natural and to some extent desirable. But if you trade in your own independence and power to rely on a woman, you will find that you have given away your most precious assets for a life of weakness. You can build a life of emotional reliance on a woman, but if you do you will be constructing a house of cards that will eventually fall apart.

Don't get me wrong. Women are great, and so is marriage. The key question is: How do you make a marriage last, and, more important, how do you make a marriage that will make you happy and fulfilled? Some answers follow.

USE YOUR MARRIAGE TO LEARN ABOUT YOURSELF

Marriage is a great teacher. Your wife is a perfect mirror for you: she will, without trying at all, push every one of your buttons. She'll bring out your fears, your old upsets and issues, things you don't want to look at, and things that unconsciously drive your behavior.

If you have an underlying fear of being abandoned and not appreciated, your wife will withdraw or demonstrate doubts about being married to you and cause you to feel insecure and afraid. If you have a desire to be private and spend time alone, you may find that your wife wants to be closer than what you consider comfortable. She will seem to instigate constant conversation.

When your old hurts surface, you'll blame, attack and criticize her and, at times, desperately want to throw in the towel and quit. How many times have you felt like leaving your marriage? Threatened it? Practically all men want to leave at one time or another. It is a constant temptation when things get really tough—and things are toughest when your emotional patterns are triggered. This is because the intense hurt and anger you feel is what you felt, or kept yourself from feeling, when you were a child. One common childhood reaction is to lash out at those who hurt you. Another is to run away to hide your hurt and pain when Mom or Dad didn't seem to love you.

Instead of running away, take notice of how this process occurs and turn it to your advantage. During the next argument, watch your emotions and the childhood reactions underneath them:

Hurt: How could she do this? I thought she loved me.

Fear: She's going to abandon me, and I'll be alone with no one to take care of me.

Anger: How dare she try to control me! I need freedom and she wants all of my power!

Try to determine where your strong reactions come from. Look back at how you felt around your childhood caregivers or authority figures. Link how your wife incites similar childhood feelings. Try this and you may discover that your bad feelings aren't really about your wife at all—they are about things that happened long ago.

I'll give you an example from my own life. One night recently my wife and I were arguing about money, specifically why she always had to pay the bills and I avoided it. At first I became angry. "Didn't she understand all the things I did for her?" After a while, I felt guilty. "You know, she's right. I don't keep track of our finances very well, and I do depend on her to pay the bills." Then I felt ashamed of how weak I was, how ineffectual. Finally, I looked deeper and I realized that the reason I did such a bad job of paying the bills was because I was afraid. I was afraid of spending too much money, of messing up. As I looked at it, I saw that was a feeling I'd carried since childhood; my dad was the authority and I was afraid of not measuring up to his high standards. My father has been dead for nearly thirty-five years, but I'm still reacting to him! Believe me, this isn't easy to see.

Like most men, I haven't enjoyed looking at childhood issues. Unlike many women I know, we men don't relish "processing" our feelings, especially out loud. We say, "Why should I spend all that time digging up old crap with my parents and the rest of my family? I want to move on—not pick at old scabs!" These reactions are normal, and occur for the following reasons:

You don't want to deal with pain—you want a comfortable, easy life and would rather avoid "looking for trouble."

You see the value of rethinking the past, at least intellectually, but are afraid to open "Pandora's box." It seems that looking at the past will allow vast amounts of unresolved, overwhelmingly bad feelings to roll in, and you would rather not deal with them because they are too unpleasant and "unproductive."

However, you risk a tremendous amount when you close off your past. If you want, you can hold on to your reservations about digging too deeply into your emotions, but if you do it will imperil your marriage and leave you with a more difficult, emotionally turbulent life. In the end, you will find it easier and more energizing to deal with your old hurts that drive current behavior. It takes way too much energy to bottle everything up for the rest of your life. Besides, you can't successfully bottle it up. When you try to hold it all in, you find that your anger, frustrations, sadness and other "leftover" feelings explode the bottle at the most inconvenient times. Those men who act like they "have it all together" rarely do! We are here on this planet to learn. Use your marriage as your primary teacher to learn what you need to about yourself so that you can become a happier person. Your marriage will always produce plenty for you to learn from.

DON'T SINK YOUR OWN BOAT

As we saw in the story of Frank and Wanda, if you hold on to your marriage like a life raft, eventually you will sink and drown, because no one—not even your wife—can ever rescue you from your own insecurity. However, if you can build an internal anchor of security, you will be a happier person and better marriage partner. Husbands often unconsciously want their wives to take care of their hurts, soothe their emotions and tell them what they feel. If you persist in using your wife this way, you will drain her emotionally and block much of her own growth and stability. You will also stay childish and immature.

Anything can happen in life, including divorce and death. There is no guarantee that any marriage will last, or that it will give you the ultimate security you may crave. Far too many people today find it easy to leave their marriages for all sorts of poor reasons, usually because they have stars in their eyes about what marriage can give them. They are disappointed, and give up before they really even try to make it work.

If you see marriage for what it really is—a testing ground to learn about yourself, grow as a human being and expand your capacity for love—you most likely will see that it's worth holding on to. You will have much less pain and have far more inner freedom if you view marriage as a living, breathing organism that needs frequent time, energy and spirit to breathe and flourish.

We have looked closely at the purpose of marriage. It's time now to return to the construction of your vision for marriage. I'm going to make a recommendation for your vision. To my way of thinking, it makes sense to start with the widest vision for marriage that you can. That way you'll never run into a dead end; you'll have an inspiring guide for almost every tough situation in which you find yourself. I have found that a great marriage vision has three vital parts.

A THREE-PART VISION

Your marriage vision needs to be big enough to inspire you to reach higher and clear enough to guide you along your way. Here are three vital components you may wish to include: taking responsibility for your internal growth, loving and respecting your mate and supporting your partner's growth.

TAKE RESPONSIBILITY FOR YOUR OWN INTERNAL GROWTH

Let's take this statement apart, piece by piece. It is your responsibility to become a better person. It's not your wife's job. The reason she criticizes your bad habits may have a lot to do with her own inner "demons." The bigger your wife's demons, the worse the criticism will be. Like many women in marriage she will project or transfer her own issues onto you, and over time you will see, with increasing clarity, when that is happening. On the other hand, she has some important observations to reveal to you. If you are able to welcome her feedback and use it to further your own progress, you will benefit enormously. For many women, when you can thank her for her insights (and really mean it) you will shock her and she will eventually resist the urge to bludgeon you with repeated criticism. Your wife will learn that you are in charge of your growth, and she isn't. And, if you genuinely desire to grow and change, you will be able to effectively absorb or deflect her criticism.

One man I know has become masterful at this. He genuinely wants to become a better person, but he doesn't obsess about it. When his wife tells him he is wrong, messed up or otherwise "competency challenged," he listens very attentively but he doesn't give away his power. It's interesting to watch him stand up to his wife and insist that she give him criticism that he can understand and utilize. He doesn't get too defensive; he just takes in what she says, thanks her and moves on. The wonderful thing is that his wife knows by now that—if it makes sense to him—he really will contemplate her feedback and then change. She also knows that he isn't going to roll over and let her beat on him. Most importantly, he has set strong boundaries with his wife. He has made it clear that he wants to hear important feedback but it has to be useful to him, not to her. His wife seems to respect him for his stance, and he continues to be responsible for his own internal growth.

Regardless of what your wife does, it is time for you to look at yourself thoroughly and honestly. Where is your life heading? What do you identify with? To some degree, all men identify with something outside of themselves: a job, sports teams, physical appearance or family, to name just a few. We try to do what society tells us a man should do—be strong, be courageous, make money, accomplish a lot, provide for our families, never show weakness, conform and especially "perform" and succeed.

As noted, men are especially cut out for battle and competition. So, we compete at work and sometimes become workaholics in the process. We compete to make money, to get ahead, to acquire possessions, to please our parents, wives, bosses or others. Often we compete to be the best at things that, in the end, may not have mattered at all.

In the U.S., and in most "developed" societies, we are told to wear a persona of strength and accomplishment while at the same time we are expected to learn to "be in touch with our feelings." However, quite a number of women and men recoil at the sight of a man who is vulnerable and in touch with his feelings. Our society gives precious little permission or rewards for men to become internally focused and sensitive. We are told to be like John Gray ("Men Are From Mars"), but we somehow get the message to be more like John Wayne. (When was the last time you saw a movie about a male hero who was vulnerable, introspective and compassionate?) We're told to be softer and more vulnerable, and when we do there are always forces ready to crush us. At least it feels that way.

How do we learn to be the "right" kind of a man? Most men learn how to "be a man" from their fathers. If husbands haven't worked through the emotional issues they carry from their interactions with a father or other male caregivers, they unconsciously follow this view of being male—however skewed it may be. We all like to believe that we are very different from our fathers but none of us escapes his influence, even if he wasn't present. From the father, we learn how to get angry, reveal softer feelings, care for children and how to hold down a job. We also learn how to treat women, whether to be devoted and idolizing of them, or to treat them shabbily. Our fathers set the pattern for us and it's up to us to build on or revise the basic architecture.

My father was a loving, strong, upstanding man who became a respected physician in the small town where I grew up. He was also a hard-working, intense man who wanted to give every-thing to his family. He grew up in the Depression and lost his father at age sixteen, and he had to help support his family as he worked his way through medical school. His experience of life was that it was a struggle against people and external forces that he couldn't control. But he tried. My dad was often angry and rigid about the "right" way to do things. I tried my best to identify with my mother, who was less angry and controlling. And I actually thought I wasn't much like my dad—until I got married. Then I was amazed to find that many of my father's behaviors came out in my interactions with my wife and kids. Have you had the same experience?

I want you to examine your relationship with your father and other important men in your life, because it will help you become strong and independent. It would be great for you to look at how you view your mother and other women, too. I know men who were surprised to discover their own "secret" thoughts that women are subservient and need to be controlled or put in their place. I've known other men who wanted the woman to be the one in control. You may think you have been free of these kinds of emotional burdens so far, but you will never be free until you see what is truly holding you down. And each of us finds plenty of emotional burdens in the way of our own happiness.

It is time for you to drop the various masks that you wear to get through life. The battles that really matter are on the inside, because if you win those you can accomplish great things in life and feel satisfied. If you don't fight the inner battles, in the end your external victories will feel empty. Marriage is the one place where you will have plenty of ammunition for the internal battles that matter.

LOVE AND RESPECT YOUR MATE

The ultimate aim of marriage is to learn to love yourself and your wife unconditionally. Your ability to truly love your wife with an open heart is directly correlated to your ability to love yourself. What you may think of as love might actually be conditional—you love her only if she pays attention to you, fixes your breakfast, mothers you and your children well and doesn't complain too much. True love desires nothing and comes from no expectations. Unconditional love develops over time and grows as your self-development matures. When you feel unconditional love for your wife, want only the best for her and give her your heart, you know you're on the way.

A good place to start learning to love at a deeper level is to develop a great friendship with your wife, one that relies upon trust and acceptance. Learn to accept her emotional troubles, hard edges and annoying habits. Acceptance breeds forgiveness, and forgiveness opens the door to love.

Every man sees parts of his wife's behavior that he dislikes. If I thought it would help you, I could make a list of things my wife does that piss me off. But the only thing that matters is whether you can live with your wife and truly accept her anyway. Don't worry if you can't accept or forgive certain things she does. We are talking about a long-term process here, not something that you do easily. You learn to love your wife by finding the place within yourself where you can love and forgive her even though she can be a pain. This takes time and it becomes integral to whether and how you will move forward in this life.

SUPPORT YOUR PARTNER'S GROWTH

Your wife is responsible for her own internal growth as well. You can support her in this process by your kind words and helpful feedback, but it's her responsibility. You cannot and should not try to control her process of change. If she refuses to change, that is ultimately her choice. Here's the good news: she will be much more likely to change for the better if she sees that you are engaged in a relentless change process of your own. And she will be more likely to change for the better if she feels your love and acceptance.

To provide the kind of support that will make a difference, you must learn to see the best in her, regardless of what side she is showing. You can become a witness to her inner and outer struggles—a confidant to her and a great "well-wisher" for her voyage through life.

Seek out, develop and commit to your vision of marriage. A "status quo" marriage will inevitably deteriorate or stagnate, while a mutually supportive marriage has a great chance to improve. Strive to create an open and supportive marriage every day. We will return to this topic again in Step Three. And while we are on the topic of learning to love and support your wife: What about love? Isn't love supposed to be the whole point of marriage? Well, yes and no. Next, we will tackle the topic of love in marriage.

THE SEARCH FOR LOVE IN MARRIAGE

One of the greatest illusions is that another person will bring us love. It is true that we may feel love when we are with people we love. But they don't give us the love or good feelings we feel—they trigger an experience of what is already there. You have terrific strength, power and love inside, at least in potential form. You also have the ability to feel compassion and caring for another person. Marriage can bring all of these great qualities out.

You can look at your life as a long expedition in which you acquire good qualities or virtues along the way. Various people and experiences bring out new feelings and characteristics, or shape old ones. For example, activities such as meditation or quiet reflection bring out peacefulness. Exercise or martial arts may reveal and develop your strength and focus. Caring for others with kindness and affection makes you more compassionate. The more you are aware of the purpose of your life journey, the more likely you will pursue activities and people that help you acquire the inner qualities you desire.

You don't have to be religious to understand that love is what you want in life. Love is a constant in the universe and accessible by everyone. Your marriage can be a wonderful path to learn to love more fully. If you could truly and fully love your wife, you would see her as being the same as you at the most fundamental level. Learning to love at deeper and deeper levels is what marriage is all about.

I want you to see love and marriage clearly and without blinders, because that's going to help you turn around your own marriage. For example: Shouldn't your wife love you? Yes, but…read on.

YOU WON'T GET THE LOVE YOU ARE LOOKING FOR FROM YOUR WIFE

If you believe that your wife has the love you want, it will color many of your interactions with her and shape the quality of your relationship. You may get too "needy" for her attention or affection. You may even worry that she doesn't love you enough, or that she is becoming too interested in other people, places or things. You may try too hard to please her or become too focused on her at the expense of yourself. If she seems to deny you the love you crave, you may get angry or resentful. The strange thing about needing love from your wife is that this need will only drive her away, denying you the very thing you want.

Conversely, the more you find love and strength in yourself, the more attractive you will seem to your wife and others. People naturally want to be around those individuals who are self-reliant, happy and centered.

Is there love in marriage? Of course! Being in a marriage can bring out deep feelings of unselfish love. Being able to fully open up, to trust another person, to commit to that individual's growth and happiness—these qualities will bring out your own innate goodness. However, if you grasp to "get love" from your wife, you will deny yourself the opportunity to grow into all that you want.

The best approach is to open yourself as fully as you can to the experience of love—that's what gives life meaning. Enjoy the experience whenever you can, and share it with your wife. But if you think you will find love from any other person, it is a mistake that will only leave you disappointed.

Here's something else that might surprise you. We all want love in our marriages. But the experience of love in marriage will deepen and become stable only through the practice of hard work, or what I call "austerities." Austerities may be defined as rigorous, difficult activities that require struggle and patience over a long time. In the U.S., and in many other Western societies, people have become conditioned to think they can receive whatever they want instantly, with little pain. Fast food, faster internet, constant stimulation—you know what I mean. But love takes work. I know that's not what you thought you were getting into when you got married; you wanted to be loved and to feel great. You got married to your woman because it felt good most of the time, and you assumed the love would always be there. If you are married you know by now that's not always the case.

The opportunities for inner work in marriage are endless. Every time you forgive your wife for a perceived or real slight you are performing an austerity just as real as the ancient spiritual seekers who had to go without food or water or stand on one leg for hours. Every time you sidestep your own ego enough to hear the truth of your wife's words about you, you are, again, performing an austerity. And, every time you accept one of your wife's faults and love her anyway you are doing the inner work.

It's difficult to love another person fully. It doesn't just happen. The truth is that real, deep love doesn't come easily except at the beginning of marriage. I sincerely hope that you have an easy time of it in your marriage. But sometimes, "love and marriage" only go together in the movies. It may take hard work and every ounce of your will to bring love into your life when times are tough. The real work of marriage is to untie the egotistical bonds that hold you. I hope you will take this journey seriously. It's one that will make your life feel worthwhile, even when you and your wife "aren't getting along."

We can turn our attention now to the issue of how commitment fits into the marriage vision. Commitment to what? For how long? Please read on.

BASE MARRIAGE COMMITMENT ON INTEGRITY, NOT DUTY

What was marriage like in ancient times? Were people "committed" to marriage?

For roughly the first three thousand years of recorded history, marriage ties were based on kinship, family and duty. Women had very little say about whom they married. Marriage was entwined with property, family and social class, and people married to satisfy the expectations of family or society. Because individual choice and freedom were more closely constrained, they probably weren't "committed" to their marriages in the way we think of the term.

After the rise of Christianity, religion played a primary role in Western marriage. The church prescribed the roles of husband and wife, the marriage ceremony, the vows and the bounds of the marriage itself, including sexuality, infidelity, property and divorce. Until the early 20th century, people married for property, safety, society or family—but rarely for love. Again, the choice of a marriage partner was limited, and most couples were committed to staying together mostly out of custom and for security.

Even today, the word *commitment* often conjures up images of being shackled or trapped into a life devoid of freedom. As you see half of marriages in the U.S. collapse, you may begin to wonder whether marriage commitment has gone the way of the buggy whip. I want you to look at the word *commitment* in a different way. As men, we inherently rebel at the loss of freedom that "commitment" implies. If we are going to make our marriages last, we need another approach.

The power that will hold you and your wife together is your own integrity—not custom, tradition, society or even guilt. Integrity, in this case, means your adherence to your marriage vision, principles and goals. Many forces in our society can act together to pull your marriage apart, but no institution or outside force can make you stay married in the 21st century. You will have to stay married only because you take a stand to stay together, and because you believe in the power of marriage to change you for the better.

If you want to be a man of integrity, you must have integrity about your marriage. Resolve to make your marriage strong, to stay together and to make your marriage a vehicle for your own growth.

COMMIT TO GROW TOGETHER,
NOT JUST TO STAY TOGETHER

The primary reason most marriages fail is that one or both spouses had impossible romantic expectations for the marriage, gleaned from fairy tales and the popular entertainment media. The 20th century ushered in mass acceptance of the idea that love is the only reason to become married. Now in most countries, couples wait to become married until they fall in love. Romantic love is exciting, fun and sensual, but it thrives on illusion and longing. Neither is a good basis for the everyday reality of marriage.

More than one hundred fifty years ago, people who expected romantic, everlasting love throughout marriage would have been ridiculed and set straight immediately by their family and friends. It was clear in those days that the primary purpose of marriage was to provide both husband and wife with economic security and to produce offspring who would help with work and/or carry on the family name.

In modern times, people in developed countries infrequently marry for security or survival, and couples seldom marry for family name or status. Most people marry for romantic love, and they expect to have everlasting romance and love throughout their married lives. The result is a great many frustrated people.

Marriage Expectations

So if you can't count on romantic love to last throughout the marriage, what should you expect? First of all, you can still enjoy some romance in your life, just learn to stop holding on to it or expecting it to always be there to feed your excitement. There is something indefinable, something wonderful that can happen between husband and wife. It comes in small moments—a little glance between the two of you, a shared memory, a tight hug at the end of the day, time in bed on Sunday morning. These are fleeting glimpses of something much larger than your usual perception. They can remind you of a deep love between the two of you, and if you appreciate these moments they can be just the sparks you may need to stay together for another day, week or year.

But these moments, because they are transitory and unpredictable, aren't enough to build a marriage around. If you've ever planned a "romantic" evening that fell flat, you know how fleeting romantic love can be. You go to the right restaurant, order the right food, take a walk in the moonlight and…your cell phone goes off. You go home, light candles, put on soft music and…your wife starts her period and has cramps. Romance can't be controlled.

What can you expect from marriage and what can you really commit yourself to? The least you can expect is that it will survive, that you and your wife will stay together. If you are truly committed to staying together you can weather many, many storms, but even that expectation is limited since it doesn't speak to the quality of your marriage. If you only want to stay together, you may hang on until you are grasping a dead marriage. One that is alive in form only. This marriage doesn't feed either party; it's merely an empty shell.

You can make the best of marriage if you commit to growing separately as well as together, and to learning how to love yourself and each another at deeper and deeper levels. You can and should have a strong preference to stay together forever. There are never any guarantees, but if you focus on the commitment to grow through marriage it will inject energy and life into the relationship and your chances of staying together will grow immensely.

One thing we haven't acknowledged is that commitment changes over time; it's not a static thing. Next, let's look at how commitment moves across time.

COMMITMENT EVOLVES OVER TIME,
AND IT CAN'T BE FORCED

Let's face it. Unless you were previously married, when you made the commitment to "love and cherish 'til death do you part" you had no idea what it meant. You may have thought you were always committed to marriage, but your commitment the first year may differ a great deal from what it is—or will be—in the seventh, fifteenth or thirtieth year.

Commitment to marriage has to evolve over time. The first stage of commitment comes after you've experienced the initial blush of marital excitement. Such a commitment is based on what you imagine marriage will be like, and it sure looks beautiful before you get into it. The reality of marriage—washing the dishes, putting away the clothes, arguing over money, etc., has yet to show its face. The first stage might last for a few weeks or a few years—but it will surely end.

The second stage of commitment occurs after you face the inevitable conflicts and upsets that happen once marriage really gets underway. Many people give up their marriage when they come to this point. Some make a temporary or conditional commitment. "I'll stay with this thing as long as the kids are young." Or, "I'll hang on until I can't stand it any longer." This is better than no commitment at all, since it keeps you together and gives you the chance for positive experiences that might well evolve into something more powerful.

Those who persevere usually grow into a commitment based on a more realistic view of marriage. This stage has frustrating power struggles and other difficulties yet offers real growth and deepening love. This type of commitment looks like, "This may be difficult, but I can see the benefit of hanging in there. I'm staying with it."

I'm amazed to look back and say that I was in this stage for well over a dozen years. It was difficult, upsetting and turbulent. Much of the time, I wasn't that happy to be married. We fought, retreated, clashed and made up—over and over and over. It was exhausting sometimes, and unpredictable always. We knew we loved each other, but we couldn't stop fighting. Yet I kept learning about how I was contributing to the difficulties. Eventually I realized I needed to listen better, and that my wife had much to offer if only I could hear her. I was thrown into a painful look at my faults: neediness, selfishness and a lot more unpleasant stuff. Over time I noticed that I was changing for the better, and that I was benefiting by staying committed to the process. But it was tough.

Commitment may look different to each person. Some have to recommit to their marriage every day or so; long-term commitments are too frightening or overwhelming. Others' personalities allow them to more easily make long-term or lifetime commitments. I am an 'all-or-nothing' person; forever commitments come easily to me. My wife, like many women, questions things almost daily. It took me a long time to allow her to be where she was in her commitments to marriage, school, parenthood and the other aspects of her life.

Eventually you may find that your commitment to marriage changes. You begin to see that you are committed to marriage as the means to become a fully developed, happy person. In that context, your marriage becomes a steady boat that you hold tightly to because you can see it taking you closer and closer to your goal on the far shore—the peace of mind and strength that you want.

I am convinced that marriage is the "fast ride." Have you ever noticed that men who aren't married look less mature than those who are married? They may be more carefree, but usually they are more in the dark about themselves. They haven't been tested; their rough edges haven't been knocked off like those of married men. Parenthood sands down quite a few more blemishes. I'm certain that marriage is the best way to advance toward maturity and self-awareness. You can be single and be Peter Pan, never settling down and always remaining a boy. But if you are married you have the opportunity to acquire true wisdom and stable love. That's worth committing to.

Your marriage commitment will, of course, undergo many trials. One of the biggest is the challenge of parenthood, so that's our next topic.

PUT YOUR WIFE FIRST AND YOUR CHILDREN SECOND

In the age of two working parents, time is at a premium. Even if one parent isn't working outside the home, he or she is likely to be constantly in motion. A parent who isn't "working" usually works harder as a housewife or househusband, with less recognition and stimulation, than the parent who is "working" outside the home. We parents come home late, tired and stressed, run out to pick up the kids from karate lessons or baseball practice, make dinner, spend a few minutes of family time and put the kids to bed. We may have only a few minutes to talk before we fall into bed exhausted. We spend weekends on errands, children's activities, home repair and social obligations and maybe a party or two. When simple survival—just getting through the day—is our objective, where is the time to spend on marriage?

The answer lies in how we see our roles as parents.

In our society, children have become almost sacrosanct. We build our schedules and lives around them and make them the focus of our families. A generation ago this was unheard of; kids fit into their parent's lives, not the other way around. We have upset the traditional and fundamental balance between parents and children—to our own detriment and theirs.

If you and your wife identify yourselves primarily as parents, you gradually lose the power and energy you generated when you got together. You also lose the transformative nature of your relationship. All the excitement and "charge" leaks out until you forget what you ever saw in each other. Marriage becomes a series of child-rearing and business chores, without the saving grace of a mature, loving, adult relationship.

Upon hearing these comments at one of my seminars, a man told the group that he and his wife had gone too far as parents. Their two children, three and five, slept in the parents' room, and all their clothes and toys were there, too, along with their video games. I asked the man when was the last time he and his wife had gotten away, even for an overnight trip. He said it had been three or four years. I told him that he and his wife had a "parenthood," but not a marriage! Not surprisingly, they were contemplating a divorce.

Too many couples focus completely on the children. When the spotlight always shines on them, children get an inflated idea of their importance. While you and your wife pour all your energy and time into them, you rob the marriage of the adult communication and interaction it needs to thrive. Many children's after-school and weekend activities are driven by their parents' need to make their kids smarter, competitive and well-rounded. It's not even the children's idea! Children won't suffer if they do fewer activities. It leaves more time for imaginative play, which is what children need to grow into creative, well-rounded adults.

BUILD A WORKING FAMILY UNIT

If you are a young father, you have a difficult challenge. You want to make money for your family and to climb in your career. I'm sure you want to be a great father for your kids, too. Your wife is probably frazzled, tired and less interested in sex than she used to be —and in the details of your life. What can you do? One man I know took matters into his own hands. He told his boss that he needed to be off at a certain time at least twice a week, so he could spend more time with his family. At least once a week he takes his wife out, away from the kids, and makes time to talk over their week and to re-connect. He and his wife have created one rule; on these occasions, they can't talk about the kids. As a result of the energy he has put into it, his marriage has been thriving.

THE GALAXY

Make your marriage the Sun and put the children orbiting around you both. If you make the marriage strong your kids benefit anyway, because you will be united in love and aligned in your approach to them. A strong marriage makes it easier to plan for, nurture, guide and discipline your children. The love and good feelings you generate will support their emotional well-being and strengthen your family. Children sense when Mom and Dad are getting along, and, without knowing why, they react poorly when you aren't.

It's really never the kids' fault if a marriage isn't working; it's the parents'. There will always be a million reasons why you can't find time to communicate, have fun or make love. You must take charge of your time and your marriage, and make it a huge priority. Children will adapt to whatever circumstance is present in their home. If they are used to receiving all the attention, that is what they will demand. If they know that Mom and Dad need time to themselves because they love each other, the children will learn to adapt to that, too, and they will receive a great model for a working marriage.

Plan regular evenings for you and your wife to relate, relax or have fun together. Spend the money to hire a babysitter. Family life can be stressful and can easily take over all your time. You need to zealously guard and arrange for "just Mom and Dad" time, and support your marriage first.

CHALLENGES

Small children present a major challenge because they require so much time and attention simply for "survival"—dressing, feeding and holding. If you are a parent with young children, you will have to adjust your schedule to find time to maintain your marriage. This means time to go out to dinner or a movie, time to talk about something other than kids and time for closeness and intimacy. You can find the time, and it's worth it.

For men, one of the first parental challenges we may face is our wife's bonding with the new baby. A mother's loving attention is biological in nature, critical to the baby's health and completely understandable. Yet it also may exclude the baby's father; this means less sex, less attention and less time together for husband and wife. During this period, it's easy for any man to feel left out and deprived. It's a natural reaction and it has happened that way for a long, long time, probably as long as humans have been around. Know that this situation will change. It may take months and it may take the first year of the baby's life, but, if you play your cards right, things will gradually turn around.

What you need to do during this period is to get stronger. You are no longer the "child" in the house, the sole target of your wife's nurturing. This is the time to take care of your own needs and learn how to be a father to your new child. Ask for what you need from your wife, but understand that she may not treat you as "number one" for a while. However, if you adjust to your new role and show patience she will come around. Meanwhile, you can enjoy learning how to be a father to a new baby in your house.

One special challenge arises when the father of children from a previous marriage has periodic custody of those kids. He may give so much extra time and attention to these children when they come to live with his "new" family that his current wife feels slighted and left out, and maybe the other kids, too. Over time this can be dangerous to the marriage and it's unfair to the new wife.

If you are in this situation, pay attention. Do you subtly side with your child against your wife? Do you give so much energy to your previous children—or, for that matter, any children in the house—

that your wife feels left out? It's up to you to set the boundaries with your children. They need to know that Daddy loves his wife and needs to spend time and attention on her too.

Whatever your parental situation, give your first allegiance to your marriage. Make time for your wife first, and keep pouring energy and love into your union. Children thrive in loving atmospheres— and so do their parents.

We've covered some of the issues men face in parenthood. Here's another: Every man is tempted by other women. Given that, it's important for you to have clarity about sexual fidelity in marriage. Next we'll look at some of the issues around that topic.

COMMIT TO FIDELITY AND
SEXUAL EXCLUSIVITY IN MARRIAGE

Fidelity is complete loyalty to your wife. When you have fidelity, your eyes may wander but your mind and heart never waver in your commitment to her. This takes work, and it doesn't come right away. Like all virtues, it takes practice to achieve. Fidelity is important because it gives you a single-minded, intense focus that offers incredible power in life and marriage. If your commitment and loyalty are to your wife you will become a stronger person with fewer distractions—one who has a better chance at maintaining a strong marriage. But if you aren't fully there yet, don't worry. You aren't alone.

It is common knowledge that men have an innate desire to have sexual intercourse. In fact, some scientists say that sexual fidelity in the animal kingdom is extremely rare—practically all animals mate with multiple partners. It seems obvious that men will be tempted to have sex with other women because of a biological desire to "scatter our seed." We will have urges to "stray" from our wives even if we don't consciously want to do so. Most men dream, fantasize and think frequently (if not constantly) about sex. In a way, sexual affairs might seem inevitable. It is up to you to develop and rely on your own integrity to stop the cycle.

In today's culture, we have unprecedented opportunities to have sexual affairs. Some men engage in "cybersex"—where they fantasize about other women, "talk" in on-line discussions and even plan clandestine meetings. Surfing the internet to look at pornography will not endanger your marriage as long as it doesn't lead to a sex addiction or to real-life sexual encounters. Cybersex becomes destructive when it crosses the line into compulsion and begins to threaten your real, everyday relationship with your wife.

Many men meet attractive, interesting women at work. With so many more women in our workplaces, we have more opportunities to form relationships that can be deeper and more intense than with our wives. In our society, sex outside of marriage seems possible and available.

Our culture emphasizes sex as the goal of life and blows up its importance to tremendous proportions in advertisements, movies, television and fashion. Watch any sports event on television. If you believe what the advertisers are selling, you will have sex with beautiful women simply by buying the right brand of beer, car or tires. Sexy women are achingly just out of reach in print and visual media and on the internet. Although many women refuse to acknowledge the obvious, these women, especially young women we see on the streets, often dress in fashions meant to arouse men's sexual interest. The last forty years have brought the rise of sex therapists, how-to videos and sex experts of every kind. We are given the explicit and implicit message: sexual fulfillment is not only important, but also necessary for life. It's an easy jump from there to conclude that if sex with your wife isn't fantastic, it's practically your duty to look for it elsewhere!

Withstanding temptation is no easy battle, and one that has been going on for thousands of years. Ancient cultures such as Greece, Rome and Victorian England evolved relatively sanctioned ways for men to have multiple sexual partners, offering a number of elaborate prices and echelons of courtesans and prostitutes. Today, prostitution still thrives but is not seen as a socially acceptable option in most countries.

On the other hand, many people in Western cultures nod and wink at extramarital affairs. Americans once punished the sexual affairs of politicians and movie stars. Fatty Arbuckle, the silent screen star, was ruined by a well-publicized liaison with a young woman. In the '50s, Ingrid Bergman's career was almost destroyed by a well-publicized affair during her marriage, and she was forced out of American films for several years. Gary Hart, the Democratic front-runner in 1988, was forced out of the race and politics altogether for a much-publicized sexual adventure during the presidential campaign. However, in recent years, American society has become increasingly tolerant of extramarital affairs. In Hollywood, affairs seem to generate positive publicity to fuel the sale of the latest movie or CD.

In private, however, a sexual affair still rips apart the fabric of a marriage and is not so easily forgiven. We know that affairs invariably hurt our partners, our children and ourselves, and endanger a stable marriage. However, part of the attraction to a new woman is that she will stroke your ego if you are feeling bored or stale with your life.

When you look in a new woman's eyes, you see a more charming, interesting, handsome version of yourself reflected back at you. This idealized, romantic version can feel very good. The trouble is that affairs rarely lead to successful long-term relationships. Approximately seventy-five percent of those who marry their affair partner end up divorced. It's tantalizing to contemplate an affair but— in addition to the home-life wreckage we leave behind—it rarely works out.

So, Is an Affair "Wrong"?

From a religious standpoint, affairs are wrong. But I am not taking a religious point of view here. The true reason to remain faithful, from my viewpoint, is because fidelity provides peace of mind and a less complicated life. This is moral behavior in the sense that "morals" prescribe a code of conduct. I am recommending the moral behavior of sexual fidelity as a practical prescription to help you create a fulfilling life. Refraining from sexual or deep emotional affairs allows you to remain focused on internal growth and change, on your family, your work and your ongoing journey toward self-acceptance and love. Having an extramarital affair is a fantasy that promises happiness and escape from the dryness and routine of your marriage, yet rarely delivers much more than shattered families and a guilty conscience. It is far more difficult, and more admirable, to stay in your marriage and attempt to improve it rather than to look for another woman as a way out.

The ancient Indian scriptures taught men about the "dharma" of marriage. The Sanskrit word *dharma* refers to the course of action that is in keeping with your highest good, the one that fits your unique path to the experience of greatness in your life. Infidelity has been considered to be against dharma. In other words, it entails a course of action that will bring you trouble and lead you off your (spiritual) path. The purpose of marriage is to find love through the interaction and support of another. In this context, affairs are off purpose. They are exciting but dangerous to your marriage and personal clarity.

WHAT DO I DO FIRST?

So what should you do if your marriage isn't working, or if you don't receive the attention, love, sex or recognition you deserve from your wife? First, commit to improve your marriage. A committed marriage forces you to put all your energy and resources into staying with one woman, and to learn the necessary life lessons to become a whole, loving person. Learn to interact more effectively with your wife by:

- Asking for what you want in a responsible, non-critical way
- Exploring your own patterns and issues with humility, courage and vulnerability
- Attempting to work things out before you look elsewhere for fulfillment

Being faithful to one woman will eventually force you to look at the difficult internal issues under the surface rather than trying to retreat from them through the excitement of an affair. Intense attraction to another woman is a sure sign that something is off in your marriage—something that needs to be tended to before you seriously contemplate a divorce.

This information aside, if you have already had an affair or even a series of affairs, there is no judgment intended here. There is no point in beating yourself up for what you have or haven't done in the past. Just pick up where you find yourself now and do your best. We are fallible creatures, and forgiveness is a necessary part of life.

As noted, I believe that you are best served by staying with your wife—except in certain untenable circumstances. Let me explain further…

IF YOU LEAVE YOUR WIFE, THE NEXT WOMAN WILL EVENTUALLY BRING UP THE SAME PROBLEMS—SO STAY WITH THE ONE YOU'VE GOT AND WORK THROUGH YOUR ISSUES

If you give up the idea that your wife's purpose is to bring you love and happiness, then you will find it easier to stay with her for the long haul. It is not her job to make you happy or take care of you—that's your job. It's also your job to understand, take responsibility for and resolve your old childhood emotional hurts and your newer, adult upsets.

Before you evaluate whether to stay in your marriage, it's helpful to look at it as rationally as you can. You can analyze your marriage around three important factors:

- **The fit between your individual values and beliefs about life**
- **The level and quality of your communication**
- **The progress you are making toward more love and strength as a person**

Among these three the hardest to change is the first, your basic values and beliefs about life. Your values and beliefs affect the way you raise your children, have sex, deal with friendships, pursue spiritual growth, spend your time, save and spend your money and much more. If you and your wife have very different values it will be more difficult over the long haul to stay together. Very few couples have the same values about everything. I know men whose wives love parties, while they prefer to stay home. Other wives love to shop and spend money and their husbands are savers. With some couples, husbands are the big spenders. Those kinds of value differences are relatively easy to surmount.

The values and beliefs that really count are those that comprise your own vision of marriage. Before you read this book, you already had a "vision" of marriage, in the sense that you had many beliefs about the purpose of marriage and what you thought should happen within it. In this book, I am suggesting an explicit set of values about marriage that lead to success. Look closely at what the two of you value. Most people I know got together because their fundamental values about life are similar. If you and your wife are reasonably aligned about the purpose and context for marriage, then I recommend that you stay together. The more clear and explicit you are about the foundational values of your marriage, the better your chances of staying together. Your odds of staying together and being happy will also increase as you improve the other two factors—your communication and your individual growth through marriage.

It's a sure bet that no matter how difficult your marriage, you married a woman who is a perfect fit for her role in your life—to show you what you need to work on to become a better, more whole person. Your wife will reveal faults and weaknesses and emotions in you that you never dreamed you had. And she is the perfect person to bring them out for you to look at. For example, maybe you want a woman who is steadfast and stable, because your mother wasn't. It's a good bet that you will match up with someone who has wide swings of emotion and who has difficulty being grounded and steady—just like Mom. Your reactions to her wavering nature are fertile ground for you to dig into. The more you blame your wife for her failings, the more you are losing chances to investigate and change your own childhood reactions to whatever instability you carried with you into adulthood.

You may fantasize about trading her in—or about being on your own, free and alone. Maybe you dream about how wonderful another woman would be. Perhaps you've already got some candidates in mind. Be aware that any woman you choose for a serious, committed relationship will eventually bring up the same challenges. Why? Because you will fall in love with women who will unconsciously recreate your unfinished childhood issues. This is the hidden secret of marriage. You marry a woman who brings up the original family issues that troubled you. And you will do the same for her.

From one perspective, marriage can seem like a prison, full of rules and restrictions on your freedom. Looked at another way, it's a goldmine rich with nuggets of inspiration and inner discovery that you can spend a lifetime exploring. The more you explore and work through what comes your way, the more love and inner stability you will develop and the closer you will feel to your wife. This process takes time and a good deal of hard work.

Have you ever wondered why some people get married four, five, six or more times? It's because they get married with the belief that "true love" with the latest spouse will keep away all the problems they experienced with their last spouse. When they get married again, they come face-to-face with the same old painful facets of their ego, and they start the trade-in process again, exchanging the old spouse for a new one, once again hoping everything will be "fixed."

Stay with the woman you've got as long as you are learning about yourself and getting your basic needs met. You will have many of the same problems with any woman you marry. You can count on it.

Remaining sexually faithful to one woman is a major challenge. Another test in every marriage is honesty. Strong marriages always have a high degree of honesty. Weak marriages feed on lies and evasions. In the next few pages, we'll investigate the topic of honesty.

STAND FOR HONESTY IN YOUR MARRIAGE

I recommend that part of your new marriage vision be to have total honesty about those things that matter in your marriage. Keeping secrets destroys a marriage, and telling the truth is an antidote to the poison of deceit. The more deception in your marriage the more you will rely on denial to keep things smooth on the surface. Or you will move through the fuel of "blind faith" (e.g., "We never talk about things, but I assume everything's fine!"). The fragile glue between you will eventually dry up and rip apart. Eventually, the truth will be told in explosive, damaging ways. Or one of you will act problems out through an affair or other destructive behaviors. If you want an honest marriage, you need to solicit and accept the truth from your wife, and you need to have the courage to speak your own truth.

If your wife says, "Do I look fat in this outfit?" I would not recommend saying, "Yes, it makes your butt look enormous!" That kind of honesty is unkind, hurtful and stupid. Honesty in a marriage means that you don't keep important secrets from your spouse, that you are open and forthright and that you don't hide portions of your life from her view. Some men keep secret bank accounts. Others have "harmless" flings. Some just have "dangerous" conversations or flirtations they don't share with their wives. Many men have feelings and dissatisfactions about their marriage or life that they are reluctant to disclose. As I've noted, many men in their marriages don't want to rock the boat; they'd rather create the appearance of ease and fluidity, even if the situation is tense and terrible.

I have learned the hard way that it's better for me to know if my wife is unhappy with me. I used to figure "no news is good news." Over time, I realized that she was keeping some of her worst feelings from me because she thought they were "unacceptable" or shameful. This caused us to get so far apart that we almost split up. When we've had trouble in the last few years, I sometimes have had to push her to tell me the full truth. The reason I do this now is that I want to know before things spiral out of control. It's so much easier to deal with things that are in the open; they lose much of their power just by being out in the light. The longer we wait, the more the issues between us acquire power.

If you lead the way in this facet of your marriage, it may not be easy. It could open up painful conversations. Your wife could get emotional, and so could you. You may end up dealing with things that you never wanted to hear—which could lead to feelings of betrayal, rage, sadness and a lot more. You can think of these conversations as essential "preventive maintenance," and sometimes as a "major overhaul." Without preventive maintenance, your car will develop problems that can cause accidents or cost you a fair amount of money in repairs later. Similarly, although everything can look shiny when viewed from the street by others, without mutual honesty your relationship can easily get into trouble. Candid discussions open up the possibility of change. Truthful, heart-to-heart conversations allow you to become more vulnerable together and thus more intimate. Intimacy brings trust and love into your relationship.

Sometimes it makes sense to think of your marriage as a separate thing, something with an existence of its own—"the marriage." You can know whether something is important enough to talk about by gauging whether it might hurt the entity called "the marriage." You can use the simple test: "Is what I'm engaged in endangering the marriage or creating a barrier between us?" For example, a simple flirtation doesn't really endanger the marriage or create a barrier between you and your wife; therefore, it's probably not worth talking about. Of course, it's easy to rationalize anything away, so you will have to do a "gut check" when looking at whether something is big enough to discuss. By all means, don't look for trouble. This is a matter of integrity and discrimination; I hope you will take it seriously.

Only you can judge whether you need to be more honest about certain areas of your life. Resolve to follow the principle of honesty and then see what happens.

Here are some key areas where you can start infusing honesty into your marriage:

A more honest, penetrating look at the past—

- Relationships with women during the course of your marriage—especially those that might have endangered your marriage.
- Past behaviors that contributed to the decay of your marriage—i.e., your lack of attention to the relationship, poor listening or unwillingness to take responsibility for some of your own issues or behaviors.
- Past activities, friends or finances you have kept hidden.

Your thoughts or feelings—

- Important, troubling thoughts, doubts or yearnings you haven't verbalized about your marriage, your wife or life in general.
- Feelings you haven't expressed out loud—resentments, anger, disappointment, longing, sadness, etc.

A more honest, penetrating appraisal of the future—

- Your fears and concerns.
- What you want and need from your wife—spoken without blame and criticism.
  - Your hopes and vision for the marriage.
    - What you will do to make your marriage better.

If you aren't sure what you feel, talk anyway and the truth will eventually come out. Learn to express your feelings about marriage, parenthood, work or other aspects of your life. Feelings can be positive or negative—it doesn't matter. Just talk. Later in this guidebook you can learn more about how to express yourself.

Please take note of three important things:

- Don't try to say everything in one sitting. Once you make the commitment to honesty, demonstrate it over time and encourage your wife to display the same level of sincerity and openness. As you show your ability to be honest, clear and without looking to blame, you will raise the level of trust and inspire the same from her.
- Speak about yourself rather than about her. When building trust through honest conversations, don't use the opportunity to attack your wife or assail her with faults. Be honest in clearing the air about yourself. If you have a transgression

to talk about, it's important that you do the inner work necessary to understand what happened and why, and to re-commit to the marriage. If you do this you won't come across as weak and sniveling. You may or may not want to ask for forgiveness, but either way you'll have some inner strength and dignity and that will come across powerfully.

- When your wife speaks honestly to you, however clumsily, do your best to listen and accept what she says without an emotional, critical response. If you punish or criticize her honesty, you jeopardize the chance for trust and honesty to thrive in your marriage. Know that her emotions are real and important for her, and that you must listen and hang in there as they come out.

To recap: make a full stand for honesty in your marriage. Over the course of several conversations, set an example by speaking truthfully and sincerely. Ask your spouse to reveal her honest thoughts, feelings and needs, too. Listen completely and refrain from being defensive or criticizing what she says. Initially, honest interactions may be painful; over time they will build intimacy and trust and will help bring you closer together.

We will conclude the discussion of your marriage vision by looking at an extremely critical issue for you: your masculine power and how masculinity manifests in your marriage.

STAND FULLY IN YOUR MASCULINE POWER (IT'S OK TO BE A MAN!)

Think of the ideal marriage as a fully charged battery with two strong poles, masculine and feminine. When your marriage is charged this way, sparks shoot out and maximum power can be harnessed for the benefit of you and your wife. If you want to have better sex, this is one way to get it. Most heterosexual men are happiest when they can fully access their own masculine energy. Repressing your essential maleness only creates unhappiness for you and your wife. Contrary to what you are told in so much of life, it's OK to be a man, in fact; I recommend it!

Male energy is our birthright, and far too many men have lost touch with their masculinity in what is in many ways an increasingly feminized society, despite the persistence of glass ceilings and the like. Men who act like men are too often criticized or shunned because they don't conform to current notions of "sensitive," "liberated" males. Male energy is different from feminine energy; men who act from their male power may not look "nice" to women or to men who buy into the notion of a "New Age" where men are supposed to hide their "less sensitive" masculine tendencies.

Watch some parents with their little boys and you will see what I mean. Boys are taught not to compete, not to be loud or aggressive, not to challenge authority. Little boys should behave. They shouldn't make too much noise. Shouldn't fight. Shouldn't be too rambunctious. Shouldn't swear. Shouldn't take chances. Shouldn't talk back. They should be polite. Should be—we all know the drill.

Yet all those things we're told not to do growing up are what strong men typically do. Male energy isn't always "nice"—it has an element of danger, of something wild and violent. The idea seemingly held by some is that men are by nature rough hewn and lack sensitivity and sophistication and that we are acceptable only if we cut off our wild, animal nature. I think this is one of the great misperceptions of the 20th (and now the 21st) century.

Of course it's a problem if little girls grow up learning to always act like "little girls," sometimes to the point of ending up with passive lives. But it's an even bigger problem if little boys are expected to act like little girls, in their childhood and later. Many of us are discovering that we can be fully human only if we first accept and fully draw on our inherent testosterone-fueled maleness. After we accept our own maleness, we can learn to understand and use feminine power as well. Men who aren't friends with their own feminine power are a danger to themselves and others. However, men who haven't made friends with their own male power will never truly know themselves.

As indicated, this is not to argue against your sometimes acting in a way that society calls "feminine." It is very possible, even healthy, that at various times a man will take a feminine role while his woman takes a masculine one. This may occur during sex, for example, when we change the identity of the "aggressor." Sometimes during arguments the man cries more and becomes more emotional than the woman. Similarly, a man might cook and wash dishes while a woman takes out the trash and mows the lawn. Today, more and more men are interested in introspection and exploring their feelings (a traditionally feminine role), and many women are learning to glory in performance, production, power and strength in politics and business, traditionally masculine domains. This is a good thing for society, leaving both men and women freer to break out of the boxes that society has assigned to them just because of their sex. And, as becomes apparent, freedom from gender stereotyping can be a good thing for marriages.

A marriage can function so long as each person is comfortable where he or she naturally lies along the masculine-feminine continuum. You will occasionally find marriages where the roles are reversed, where the man seems more "feminine" and the woman seems more "masculine." And nothing wrong with that. As long as one person in the marriage utilizes masculine energy or power and the other feminine, a marriage can work well. However, I recommend that you avoid meeting your wife in the middle, in a nebulous "neutral" zone. In this kind of marriage, each partner attempts to pretend that the two are the same, that men and women aren't different. These marriages, especially when one fails to follow one's own nature, can create misery for the people involved, and I don't want you to go there.

It is not my wish to draw hard and fast guidelines regarding what "should" happen along masculine-feminine lines. What I am suggesting is that in most cases a man must find his true masculine power and bring that to his marriage and other aspects of his life. Emasculated men aren't very attractive to their spouses, and I can tell you for sure that they have less sex with their wives. Men like these bring little fire and passion to their marriages. I want you to be a strong, powerful man and bring that fire to your marriage.

EXPANDING FROM MASCULINITY

A recent marriage phenomenon is the female breadwinner, masculine in her aggressive approach to life and work, and the feminine man, nurturing children and wife as a "homebody." I believe that a heterosexual woman who has enhanced her masculine energy at the expense of her feminine energy will eventually find growth through becoming more feminine, at least in some areas of her life. Feminine energy is her birthright, and if she wants to grow and blossom, she will have to explore it fully and balance her overused masculine side. Similarly, a super-feminine woman would find it beneficial to enhance her masculine side so as to be assertive and make her mark on the world.

Similarly, heterosexual men who are inclined to the feminine must eventually find their masculine core and act as a masculine presence because that is their true nature. It's fine to be a "sensitive man," but feminized, sensitive men need to bring out the full power of their own masculinity to be complete and send healthy sparks flying through their marriage. Similarly, if you are a traditional, masculine man and you reject or repress your own feminine side, you will miss out on a great deal of life and fear feminine energy in others—both men and women.

Most men instinctively fear feminine attributes, such as the ability to listen, empathize, intuit, share, cooperate, be artistic and nurture others. We were taught to feel that way despite even other important feminine influences in society. We grow up learning that if we show weakness, the kids at school or our fathers or other men and women will correct us, even shame us for not "acting like a man." Like male children for thousands of years, we have been "bred for battle," even if there is no war to fight. We learn to compete, dominate and hide our feelings and our "weaker" side from other men—and from ourselves.

When we do this, we lose access to our own feelings and intuition that come from familiarity with accessing our feminine side. When we see other men who are "different"—homosexuals, artists, "sensitive types"—we may instinctively shy away and reject them in our thoughts, beliefs and actions because we haven't accepted our own feminine side.

Your life and your marriage will work best if you explore and integrate both your masculine and feminine sides, while understanding and appreciating your basic masculine nature. Your wife will have to explore what being feminine means for her—that's surely something you are not equipped to handle.

Now, how can you be masculine within the context of marriage? Let's look at that next.

WHAT DOES IT MEAN TO BE "MASCULINE" IN A MARRIAGE?

As you might know, the answer has changed many times throughout history. It's easier to see what isn't truly masculine—neither the old, macho super-masculine male nor the soft "New Age" guy who exalts the feminine over all else. In the middle is a fully masculine male, alive with energy and connected to his essence.

For convenience, I'll describe three types of men spanning a continuum—from a traditional, old-fashioned masculinity to an evolving masculine presence to a soft, feminized man. In reality men do not necessarily fit easily into these categories, but the labels may be useful for discussion's sake. Here are descriptions of three types of males:

THE SUPER-MASCULINE MALE

This man is macho and aggressive. He clings to a rigid, traditional marriage and believes the man has all the answers. He is dominant and feels that a woman's role is as homemaker and caretaker. A super-masculine male also fears anything feminine in himself, remains "armored" against his own emotions and in most circumstances is unwilling to listen to his wife or be vulnerable and authentic.

THE FULLY MASCULINE MALE

This male seeks and emphasizes masculine energy and power: raw, earthy, sexual and strong. He is clear about his convictions and commitments and acts upon them. The fully masculine male enjoys being male and being with men. He is engaged with life and personal growth, respects the feminine in himself and in women and is willing to plumb to the depths of his darker emotions. The fully masculine male consciously emphasizes and honors masculine energy for himself, and feminine energy for his wife.

THE SOFT MASCULINE MALE

This "sensitive, New Age guy" (sometimes called a "SNAG") exalts the feminine at the expense of his own masculine energy. He thinks that feminine energy is "spiritual" but that male energy is not. The soft masculine male has no zeal for life, is often passive and tolerates only "good" emotions. He wants to avoid looking at any of his own emotional problems and prefers to jump ahead to what he considers "spiritual." In marriage, he may abdicate power to the woman and is often too "nice" for his own good.

We can also make some judgments about how these types of men would contribute to and shape their marriages. Here is what each type of man is likely to produce in a marriage:

THE SEPARATE MARRIAGE— FROM A "SUPER-MASCULINE" MAN

This marriage is hollow. It typically has little closeness, intimacy or vulnerable, honest communication. Each partner may be focused on his/her work-life, hobbies or the children. Each may have many separate pursuits and friends and may spend an inordinate amount of time away from his or her spouse. Boundaries in this type of marriage are strict—there are many implicit rules about what they do or don't do in the household, and they revolve around what men and women "should" do. This marriage is functional, patterned, even business-like, and may last a long time if expectations for love and closeness are low.

THE MERGED MARRIAGE— FROM A "SOFT MASCULINE" MAN

If you see a couple wearing identical outfits in public, they are probably in this category. This couple spends most of their time together, often in apparent harmony. Conflicts are avoided. But the wife criticizes and nags her husband while he responds with passivity or passive aggression. The couple seems "merged"—similar interests, similar attitudes, even similar facial expressions. Personal boundaries are confusing or non-existent. The couple seems most focused on "we" issues at the exclusion of their individual growth. The husband may be reluctant to leave his wife for more than a very short while and he spends little time with other men.

THE ALIVE MARRIAGE—
FROM A "FULLY MASCULINE" MAN

This marriage is based on mutual growth. The man is respected for being masculine and the woman for being feminine. The couple has a balance of together and apart time. Along with mutual friends for both, the man has his own male friends and the woman has female ones. On the other hand, when the couple is together they often communicate with trust, vulnerability and intimacy. Their sex life stays lively and expressive of their individual power. Their boundaries are clear. Each person is responsible for his/her own feelings and needs yet feels comfortable requesting what he/she wants from the other. The man feels comfortable in his masculinity, and the woman enjoys being feminine.

Being fully masculine is the last piece of your marriage vision. Take the complete marriage vision and make it your own. Change it as you see fit. Keep your mind and heart on it, and share it with your wife. It will become your pole star, the way you'll orient your journey to the married life you want to create. Now, let's move on to the second of our three steps.

CHAPTER THREE

Step Two: Take Responsibility for Your Own Issues

WHERE ARE YOU GOING?

Where are you going in life? What do you want to get out of it? One thing's for sure: We can choose what we strive for in life. I know people whose top priorities are acquiring nice things. They have a great house, fine-looking car, expensive furniture and fashionable clothes. Yet they aren't any happier than anyone else I know. I used to visit a couple who bought a huge house with a pool in one of the more expensive places in the Bay Area. I was jealous of them until I noticed that they fought all the time and that their daughter seemed miserable. It was clear to me that they were much less happy than I was, even though they had much more money and things.

We get so many crazy messages about how to be happy. We are told that good sex is the key to life's happiness. It isn't, although we can certainly enjoy it. No matter how wonderful the activities, the friends we have, trips we take or parties we go to, they can all fall flat. We just can't count on them to make us happy. We go to the beach expecting to be happy and we can get sunburned or end up with sand in our picnic lunch. At a great party we suddenly feel lonely and melancholy. You take a great vacation and end up fighting with the wife and kids.

What about our work? For men, work may seem like the key to happiness and gratification—and it can be a source of pleasure and growth. But by itself it's not enough. Promotions come and go; raises make us feel good only long enough to get the money to the bank. Many of us thrive on the challenges of our careers. But what about our home lives? The boredom, conflicts and challenges are always there waiting for us when we return from fighting the dragons.

Society teaches us that finding the right mate will give us lasting joy. You and I know that isn't necessarily true, either. One day you're thrilled to be with your wife, the next she appears to be put on Earth only to make you feel wretched. Let's face it. Women can make you feel insane sometimes.

I've learned this the hard way: the only way to withstand the craziness of marriage to a woman is to learn how to be stronger and more complete within myself. For a long time, I rose and fell according to my wife's moods. If she was angry and bitchy, I would react angrily. If she was hurt and lonely, I'd feel upset and try to make her feel better. If she rejected me, I'd feel desperate and unloved. Over time, I realized that my reactions were all about me, not her. I finally learned that it was my responsibility to become emotionally stable enough to stop reacting to her. I resisted it for a long time, but I found that there was only one way to do that: I had to learn more about my inner life, my emotional patterns and conscious and unconscious issues. That way, I could deal better with any emotional upheaval that came my way, whether from my wife, my career or my children.

I have discovered that to have meaning my life must be about my psychological, emotional and spiritual growth. The paths to these ends are many—each of us must find his own way. Once we commit our lives to inner growth, our choices change automatically, as does the course of our lives. I am urging you to make this commitment to yourself because I know it will change you for the better. Another thing that will change for the better is your marriage. Please read on to learn more about how you can take this step to improve your marriage.

TO HAVE A MEANINGFUL LIFE AND MARRIAGE
MAKE YOUR TOP PRIORITY YOUR OWN INNER GROWTH

When you make personal growth and learning your major priority, many good things will come to you. Here are some:

You will have more power and confidence at work, home or in other areas of your life, because you will know yourself better and your ego won't trip you up as much. How many times have you messed up a customer interaction or work meeting because of old emotional problems or tendencies that rear their head at the wrong time? You lost your temper or got your feelings hurt. You felt inadequate in a situation that you knew you could have handled. Why? The only way you can know is to do the work to find out. When you finally get to the root of your own difficulties in life, they will begin to clear up and you will have more freedom and power in every situation. Even when you encounter difficulties, you will use them to learn more about yourself rather than to wallow in self-pity.

You will create separate, healthy boundaries with your wife. You will learn which are your issues and which are hers. After a while you won't unconsciously treat her as your mother or father as often, and if you do you'll take responsibility for it. And you will find it easier to keep your distance from her when you need to.

You will become more loving and accepting in your marriage. The more you know yourself, the less control your ego asserts over you. The less your ego pollutes things, the more your natural, loving self will emerge. You will gradually become less judgmental, critical and argumentative; you will become a better marriage partner and find it easier to get along with your wife.

You will eliminate much of the need for your wife to criticize you. Why does your wife criticize and complain about your behavior? First, it's her nature to want to make you "better." Second, when she doesn't see you change following her criticism, she may well think her only choice is to do it again—louder and more stridently. When you take on your own inner exploration, you can stop her criticism in its tracks by your behavior. You'll listen, reflect on what she's saying and decide whether to change or not, because it's your territory, not hers! In this way, you'll get a lot of your power back from your wife.

You already know that your wife is not responsible for your feelings or for your betterment. You are. It's just that it sometimes feels otherwise. Her true role in marriage is one that you might have overlooked. What every wife inherently is good at is to help you learn about yourself. In other words, your wife's role in marriage is to trigger the demolition of your harmful, habitual patterns and beliefs. You may see this as a curse rather than a blessing, because it hurts so damned much when you are in the middle of power struggles, arguments and other ego entanglements. But if you choose to *use* her criticisms or the difficulties of marriage, they can really be a gift to you. We will investigate this idea later, but first we need to once again face our old friend, the ego.

TRICKS OF THE EGO—GETTING TO THE TRUTH

The ego is tricky. It will tell you that you are just fine the way you are; that you don't need to change a thing and that anyone who tries to tell you differently has the problem. It will tell you that if you have an argument with your wife, it surely is her fault—she should just mind her own business! However, there is another approach: you can use the argument as fuel for courageous inner exploration.

Once you get used to this point of view, your arguments and other interactions start to change. Let's say you are having a fight with your wife. It starts out simply enough. You aren't loading the dishwasher to her satisfaction, so she takes over the job. In other words, you are wrong again! You steam silently for a minute, then explode. "If you are such an expert about the dishwasher, you can load it yourself! Why do you criticize me about everything? Do you think it really matters how the damned dishwasher looks? No matter what I do, you'll find something wrong in it!"

At first, you think your anger is about her, and you blame your wife for a while. Then, you see your reaction has more to do with you. You had a hard day, and you just needed some understanding and love at home. As you think about it more, you may well discover that your anger and other feelings are really directed at your parents and what they did to you "way back when." Maybe you recollect that your mom or dad was highly critical of you when you were a kid. As you reflect on the issues further, you begin to take responsibility for your emotions and challenges with your parents, and you decide that it's pointless to blame your wife for what you didn't receive as a child. Eventually, this cycle becomes a pattern for future interactions, and you train yourself to spot your typical reactions more quickly and to take responsibility for them sooner.

The process may take minutes, weeks, months or years, depending on the issue and your desire to explore it. If you undergo this kind of internal investigation, you will find that you get to know yourself better and become a happier, more energetic person. Life is hard when your internal patterns are in charge, but it gets a lot easier when you take control and discover your own power to break the patterns. In a few pages, we will look at some of the tools and methods you can employ to help you with this practice.

I urge you not to stand pat. Make a commitment to make your life one of growth, change and inner exploration. When you do, your marriage, as noted, will become the perfect vehicle for growth; it will supply you with the fuel you'll need for your own expansion. And if your wife joins in the journey and pursues her own growth, you will have the strongest base possible for a lasting marriage that is full of love and respect. Let me tell you about a friend of mine who refused to take this journey.

WHEN RESISTANCE TO CHANGE BACKFIRES

Robert was a great father with two small children and a loving wife. It was easy to see that he was the "strong, silent type." He had an impassive face and rarely showed much emotion. I remember once I visited him and his wife after I'd been to an emotional movie. As I told him about my crying in the theater and how much sadness I still felt after the film, he looked at me like I was from Mars. Robert had a very hard time talking about what he was feeling, what he wanted from his wife and pretty much anything else that was going on "inside."

His wife was an energetic woman and a loving mother. She began advancing in her career and developed a passion for ice-skating. She found new friends and a new, male ice-skating partner while Robert stayed home watching sports on TV or playing with their two children. Soon Robert and his wife began fighting. She wanted a more alive, interesting husband, and he wanted things to be like they used to be—quiet, safe and predictable. Robert refused to open up about his feelings, or to enter counseling with his wife.

She stuck with him for two more years, begging him to loosen his grip on his rigid ideas and to work with her to save the marriage. Robert stuck to his guns. He told his wife she was all wrong—too critical and too pushy. He didn't want to open up and he didn't want to look at his feelings, wherever they were hidden. She should just leave him alone! She did. She left him and took his kids, too, and Robert lost what he cared about most.

Robert was a good person and a great father. His Achilles heel was that he just didn't want to look at himself. Maybe it was too painful for him to pierce his suit of armor. Maybe he just didn't know how. Or maybe he never saw any reason to explore his inner life. Use Robert's example. If you want to be happier, point your life in the direction of understanding and mastery of your inner demons.

Everybody has their inner emotional patterns that cloud their minds and get in the way of their enjoying life. However, most people don't want to deal with them.

If you want to grow and become stronger, you will see that you already own a built-in spiritual and psychological growth machine that will show you the areas for your own personal growth—it's your marriage. If she is willing (and most women are), your wife can become your trusted ally in the process of your own self-discovery. This is a lifelong pursuit, and it will make your life worth living.

If you are willing to tackle this job, I can guarantee you that it will dramatically change your relationship with your wife and your whole experience of marriage. For one thing, you'll hear a lot less criticism. In the next few pages, I'll tell you how you can achieve that...

DEAL WITH YOUR WIFE'S CRITICISM: TAKE RESPONSIBILITY FOR YOUR OWN GROWTH

Your wife saw your potential when she first got to know you, and she sees it even now. No matter who you were or what you had going for you when you met her, she saw areas for improvement. In her eyes, you were a remodeling project, a cosmetic fix-up or a complete re-building job. Men, of course, don't think this way. When a man marries a woman, he pretty much accepts the way she is. Our attitude is, "What you see is what you get." Or, "Don't fix me and I won't fix you." Although we know our marriage partners aren't perfect, we wouldn't dream of trying to change them, and we assume they'll feel the same way about us. This is far from the truth. Women think of you the way you could be. And as you undoubtedly know, most women spend a large portion of their married lives attempting to make their husbands better. They see the gap between where you are now and where they think you should be. You can work with this tendency or against it, but you can't change it. If you fully value this propensity of your wife to see your potential and everything that keeps you from it, you can work with it for your own betterment.

Each woman has natural and easy access to the universal feminine energy, which comes with unique feminine powers. Cultures throughout history have described aspects of the feminine powers. One of particular interest here is represented by the fearsome Hindu goddess Kali. Kali is portrayed as extremely dark; her powers come out of the infinite space of night. Her hair is disheveled, her tongue protrudes and her fearsome teeth are sharp as fangs. Blood drops from her mouth. In ancient tales, Kali destroyed demons to save righteousness and then danced in celebration on her husband's body.

It is said that she became so overjoyed with the feel of the demons' flesh under her feet that she continued dancing more and more wildly, until she finally realized that her husband, Shiva, was underneath her and that she was dancing him to death! Does this sound like your wife at times?

The name "Kali" comes from the Sanskrit word *kala*, or time. She is the power of time that devours all through death, yet she is beyond time. Kali is said to be found in the cremation ground amid dead bodies. She is often pictured standing on the prostrate body of her husband, Shiva, and she is the manifestation of Shiva's power and energy. Shiva can function only through her creative energy, and she can function only through him. Kali is one manifestation of Parvati, Shiva's wife, and so in Hinduism Shiva and Kali are linked as a couple.

We can see Kali as a doorway to understanding women. Kali is one form of the Mother Goddess, and she represents the most powerful of the female forces in the universe—the powers of creation and death. Although Kali smashes evil as a warrior goddess, she is also respected as a protector, as the great nurturing Mother of all. We can understand that all women, in earthly ways, have great creative powers, including the power to give birth, the power to nurture and protect and the power to destroy. Like Kali, women have the capacity to create terrible destruction. A woman can be extremely fierce and destructive, in a way that seems foreign and terrifying to men. Like Kali, a woman can criticize and smash a man's ego, destroying duplicity, pretension and negativity in her wake. This is a power to be reckoned with, to be respected and honored.

The power of Kali is the power that a woman unleashes when she turns her attention to the improvement of her man. Therefore, it's understandable that a man would tend to shrink or turn away from the assault. It feels uncomfortable, strange and scary when a woman turns her criticism dial to "attack mode" and starts in on you as her target. Remember, this is a natural power of women; resist it and you may be flung aside by Kali's wrath. Resist it and your wife will only come back with more ferocity.

We must honor the power of Kali because we must honor all the aspects of feminine energy in ourselves and in women. We must also respect it because if we work with it, it can uncover the aspects of our ego that need to be revealed and changed for our own good. Through a shift in your attitude, you can use your wife's criticisms to help you discover and unfold the hidden aspects of your ego. This works only if you take charge of the process of your change, rather than grudgingly ceding it to your wife.

When you see and hear the Kali energy arise in your wife, it should be a warning to you: take it seriously. Don't look away. Work with this power of destruction; get behind the process of rooting out habits and tendencies that you don't really need. But don't give your wife the responsibility to change you. "Kali energy" flows through her easily. However, every man has the responsibility and ability to wrestle and destroy his own demons. In other words, you can use your wife's power to illuminate and help you, yourself, destroy the various demons within you; however, the job cannot be done without your own command and muscle. Whether your wife helps or not, it is completely up to you to confront and overcome your inner challenges. This is the way of strength and growth and mastery in your life.

If you relinquish the responsibility and control of your own change to your wife, you lose her respect and your own. You start to feel, and appear, weak and worthless if you believe every criticism that comes from your wife. She will seem to have the corner on the truth about you; and if either of you believes she's in charge, your relationship will suffer. Subtly, you'll put her in a position of power that she shouldn't have. Not only that, you will start to resent her for constantly picking on you. Over time, you will start to tune her out and become more distant and less respectful.

This is a frequent complaint of women. They grumble endlessly about how little their men listen to their criticism and feedback, how much they resist their efforts to "help." Wives eventually start to resent what they see as "carrying" their husband's inner development. As such a pattern continues, men feel increasingly weak and worthless. Some, at the extreme, seek to reinvigorate their image by becoming the bully, pushing the woman around and abusing her verbally or physically, in some instances ending up with a woman in the hospital. There is never any excuse for such behavior; of course the increasing sense of powerlessness that many men feel—and the sometimes violent recourse that some men resort to—is hardly a rational response. Clearly, a prolonged sense of weakness, of not being oneself, of not obtaining satisfaction in life—this in itself can be sufficient to wreck a marriage.

TAKE OVER THE JOB

It's time for you to take over the job from your wife, no matter how capable she may seem. She may take vast pride in her ability to monitor your foibles and to puncture your pretenses. She may even believe that she can change and mold you until you satisfy her. The truth is that real change is a solo act; no one can do it for you but you. Of course your wife may be astounded, incredulous, even angry when you take over the responsibility for your own development, and when you begin to gently push her away from the task.

When I began to dive into my own inner emotions and patterns, I actually started to ask for feedback and to listen carefully to what my wife had to say about me. She was shocked. She also was relieved that she finally was off the hook for the job. At first she didn't believe that I really would take over. She was so good at the task and had spent years studying my imperfections! How could I do it as well as she? It took a while to convince her that I was serious about the job of looking at myself. But it turned out that all I had to do was sincerely listen to her feedback, thank her and move on. As a consequence, the criticism conversations got shorter and shorter and less rancorous. Even now I have to remind her on occasion that although I value her feedback, I'm in charge of me—she's not.

If your wife wants to give you criticism or feedback for your change process, do this: listen and thank her for the contribution to your learning. Ask questions to make sure you understand her criticism or feedback. Here's the most important thing: you have to want to hear what she says. Then you get to decide whether you will use it. If you do want to hear it, you'll listen and ask the right questions naturally and she'll know that you're serious. If the time isn't right for you to really hear her, tell her that you want to know more about her views but you need a few minutes or hours before you can hear it. It's OK if you get defensive for a moment or two, but stop yourself as soon as you can from making excuses or denials. Remind yourself that you are in charge of your own development. Make it clear by your actions that you've taken on the entire job of your emotional, psychological and spiritual progress. Then do the work to make that true. If you follow my guidelines here you'll have an easier, less contentious marriage and you'll hear a great deal less criticism at home.

I'd like to turn your attention now to another facet of your marriage—power struggles. Every marriage has them. But where do they come from? And how do you stop them? To answer those questions, we will have to look at how things changed for you and your wife from the beginning of your marriage to where you are now. Do you remember those happy, love-filled early days of romance? Let's look at them again and try to determine what happened.

THE THINGS YOU LOVED HER FOR AT THE BEGINNING DRIVE YOU CRAZY NOW—AND THAT HAS MORE TO DO WITH YOU THAN WITH HER

It's funny how things can change. At the beginning of their marriage five years ago, Will saw his wife, Laurie, as someone who was attractive, well-organized and detail-oriented. Now he sees her as a "control freak," constantly cleaning and moving every object in the house. Her cute habit of talking so animatedly about the day's activities increasingly annoys him, as it seems she never shuts up when he just needs some peace and quiet. Laurie's modern musical tastes were great when they started out—she kept him from being stuck in the past. Now, Will can't stand the sounds of hip-hop that blare from their bedroom.

Lying in bed late one night, Will mulls over the situation. *Maybe we aren't that great of a match after all,* he thinks. *What do Laurie and I have in common anymore?*

The more Will thinks about it, the more he wants to do something about it. But what can he do? He thinks about what it would be like to move out, get his own space. Nah, it hasn't gotten that bad yet. Talking it over is out; he tried that a couple of weeks ago but that was a real disaster and ended in one of their worst fights ever. Maybe he can spend more time out of the house, join a men's softball league or work more on the computer at night. Perhaps he's been working

too hard and just needs to slow down. A vacation together might
do the trick!

What Will is not seeing is that his wife hasn't changed that much.
What has happened is that the initial "easy love" phase of the
marriage—when acceptance and forgiveness arose spontaneously—
ended a long time ago. What has taken its place is the natural
process of his ego reasserting itself through judgment, irritation, criticism and righteous indignation about other people—in this case,
his wife. This is true for all of us. "Easy love" dies down and the real
work of marriage begins.

Now let's rewind and start this scene over. This time, let's see
what happens if Will sees his own reactions and moves past
blaming and accusing his wife.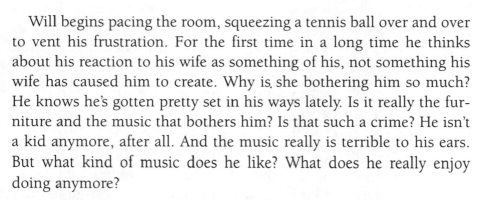

Will begins pacing the room, squeezing a tennis ball over and over
to vent his frustration. For the first time in a long time he thinks
about his reaction to his wife as something of his, not something his
wife has caused him to create. Why is she bothering him so much?
He knows he's gotten pretty set in his ways lately. Is it really the furniture and the music that bothers him? Is that such a crime? He isn't
a kid anymore, after all. And the music really is terrible to his ears.
But what kind of music does he like? What does he really enjoy
doing anymore?

Will wonders, not for the first time, why he isn't having much fun
in his life. And then another thought strikes him: Can it be that he
is really jealous of his own wife? She seems to be having a lot of fun.
She is always trying new things. It occurs to him that maybe he's
been trying to control her, to make her more like him. But why
would he do something like that?

Will paces even faster. Suddenly he stops. Is he scared of change? Is that why he resents her new music? Then another thought hits him. Is he scared of losing Laurie? Is that why he is so short with her and angry with her talking so much? Will sits down on the bed and sighs. He is aware of a constricted feeling in his chest and some sadness. He wants to connect with her again, that he knows. The stupid music and furniture moving and all the rest aren't the point at all. The point is his own frustration with his life. Will gets up from the bed again and starts for the door. He is fearful, but he walks with purpose. I'd better have a talk with Laurie and apologize, and talk it over, he thinks...

———————————

In this version of the scene, Will has discovered the horrible, splendid truth: whatever you find awful, upsetting and wrong about your wife is really a reflection of something about you. As the old saying goes, whenever you find yourself pointing a finger at your wife, look at the four pointing back at you. When you point the finger back at yourself, you will find that your wife may be guilty of bad behavior and even bad intentions, but your reactions and feelings are actually all about you.

One person can dramatically influence a relationship for the better, but only if that person has done the homework necessary to see where his issues end and the other person's begin. If you talk to your wife about something that she "does wrong," you had better be prepared to look at what is going on with you around that issue. Otherwise, all you will do is create more problems for yourself and more unending arguments.

Next, let's look at the "easy love" phase of a relationship to which I just referred. In the next several pages I'll present an answer to the Supremes' musical question, "Where Did Our Love Go?"

YOU CHOSE YOUR WIFE BECAUSE YOU BELIEVED SHE WOULD MAKE YOU WHOLE

Before you got married, you were probably euphoric about the wedding and your life beyond. How lucky you were to find such a great person, the best woman in the world for you! She was lovely, smart, and you just felt happy to be around her. It was as if a cloud of protection and grace surrounded the two of you, and no one else could ever know the feeling of that kind of accepting, all-encompassing love.

Sometime after the wedding, things slowly began to change. You started to see her faults more clearly—and she yours. In fact, she criticized and corrected you frequently. You never knew you had such faults! Why was she always bitching at you? Worse, she seemed to withhold the love and attention she so easily offered before. You felt hurt and angry. Why couldn't she see what she was doing? So you began to criticize, demand and attack her as well. Gradually, you both locked into a painful power struggle of mutual blame and recrimination. What happened to your love?

Maybe it didn't happen exactly this way...but variations of this story play out in practically every marriage. Each of us instinctively chooses a person he believes will heal the problems and wounds of his childhood—and for a while it feels as if we are healed and whole. In a way, every man believes unconsciously that his wife will become his new, and better, parent and that she will supply the feeling of being complete and whole that he lost somewhere along the way. In this sense, and in others, we do "marry our parents." Take a moment now and remember how you felt when you were accepted and loved as a child. Some of us had this experience of protection, safety and love frequently, some of us infrequently or never. Think of those times when you knew you didn't have to worry because you'd be taken care of and protected. You were loved and you felt safe. If you never had it, think of how badly you wanted it. Do you see how you wanted to create, or re-create, that experience with your wife?

Here is the bad news: it's only a fantasy that your wife will bring you everlasting love. The wonderful feelings you experienced at the beginning of your relationship came about because you temporarily felt "at home" with your true self, but these feelings are fleeting. Loving your wife fit old, familiar patterns of love from your earlier life, and with the addition of a healthy dose of illusion, you felt blissfully in love.

You will feel truly whole when you have done the work necessary to clear negative thinking and unconscious patterns out of your mind and psyche. Marriage certainly can yield feelings of companionship, love, security and intimacy. And it's possible that a close marriage can bring you and your wife to an experience of true, unconditional, unselfish love. However, as long as you rely on your wife to satisfy all of your desires and heal all of your childhood wounds, you will feel angry at her and disappointed in your marriage. I know you probably aren't aware that you want all of this from your wife, but I've never seen a man or woman yet who didn't want this out of his or her marriage, unless he or she was in a true "marriage of convenience." I know I've often wanted my wife to make me feel complete and contented, and at times I still do. As a consequence, many times I'm very disappointed.

What matters most now is what you do about the power struggles between you and your wife. Most marriages end because couples can't get past the clash of their two egos. They blame and fight each other until nothing is holding them together except their mutual recriminations. I'm going to show you how to create something much better. The place to start is with your own beliefs and attitudes about and expectations for marriage.

It's important that you realize that your wife is a human being, just as you are. She did not marry you to satisfy your needs or to give you the love you want or to make you feel whole. You can't expect any woman to make you feel safe and intact. Your best bet is to use the difficult parts of your marriage as learning experiences to help you become a better, more whole person. You do this with your wife, not because of her. Ironically, you will get the love you want in your marriage by not expecting it from your wife.

We have touched on the subject of childhood memories and their influence in your present-day marriage. It's time now to go back and learn more about how your childhood plays a part in your marriage.

WE MARRY TO HEAL OUR CHILDHOOD INJURIES AND TO LEARN

Daniel gripped the steering wheel hard—so hard that his fingers hurt. His head was throbbing, he was having trouble breathing and his thoughts were churning as he headed home from work exhausted, angry and hurt. He remembered how his boss overlooked the great job he had produced over the last several weeks, and even publicly recognized another man for doing very little! This always happens! But he can't quit because he needs the money, and transfers are impossible. Daniel hardly noticed the traffic, stoplights, the deepening dusky light or the bleating radio…he sighed deeply. He couldn't take any more.

Daniel thought of Fran at home, and the kids waiting for their daddy. He desperately wanted Fran to appreciate what he was trying to do for them. He really needed her understanding today—no challenges, no fights, no conflicts. Their fights had been escalating, and the kids seemed to be acting out the tension between them with their own tantrums. Daniel had married her because he thought she would be different from the other women—not such a self-centered bitch. He remembered his mother's absences; even when she was home she wasn't really there for him. Somehow, she never showed him that he was a major priority. Fran seemed to be different. At first, she would welcome him home with open arms. She would hug him and fix him dinner and listen sympathetically to his complaints. He guessed she had started to change when she became pregnant with their first child. She seemed to lose interest in his daily struggles. All of a sudden he wasn't so important anymore. That's when the fights began, too. They fought over everything from money to childcare duties to in-laws.

Daniel thought Fran loved him but didn't even see the real him anymore—or care about the sacrifices he was making for their family. He gave his life to them and they just took what he gave without a drop of appreciation. It was just the same with his boss! Nobody gave a damn about what he did for them. Daniel abruptly found himself on his street and pulled into the driveway. He sat there for a moment, staring at the dashboard. He was full of hurt, angry feelings as he opened the back door and looked inside for his wife…

Daniel is surely moving toward an argument. His wife probably will disappoint his expectations for love and appreciation, for she has her own issues and demands that get in the way of giving him what he wants and needs during a vulnerable time. He is locked into feelings that originated a long time ago, and things will only get much worse if he doesn't see the pattern. Daniel, as with all of us, carries his childhood injuries and acts them out with his loved ones. His experience of being unappreciated and unacknowledged is re-creating itself in his family life—and he will blame other people for his own unmet needs.

Here's what Daniel should do: notice that practically every time he feels upset, angry or sad about Fran's lack of attention and love he is actually upset, angry or sad about his mom's lack of attention and love. He can begin to stop blaming Fran for not giving him what his mother couldn't give him. Daniel needs to dig into his bad feelings about his mother and somehow start to heal them. Most of all, he needs to be accountable for his own feelings and start to work through them, rather than acting them out in damaging ways with his family.

HOW OUR PARENTS AFFECT OUR MARRIAGE

It is often said that we "marry our parents," and (in a way) that is true. If you look closely, you will probably find that your wife has many of the traits (positive and negative) of your parents or other caregivers. Even though she may differ from them in significant ways, at times when you are with your wife you will experience or "re-create" the way it felt to interact with your mother or father. For example, if your father was too critical of you, you may see your wife as being critical sometimes, when she actually is trying to help. Or you will judge and criticize your wife, just as your father did with your mother.

The woman we marry literally "fits our pictures" of our parents—primal impressions we carry with us from childhood. The actions and emotions simply feel similar to Mom or Dad, and that's why it feels so good—and so bad—to be with your wife. According to Harville Hendricks, author of *Getting the Love You Want*, when we marry we set up a new "father and mother" experience, then we unconsciously re-experience many of the same emotional patterns that drove our parents' behavior as well as our own when we were children.

You probably didn't know it but you got married partly because you believed, unconsciously, that your wife would "re-parent" you and that this time you could heal what got hurt the first time around. If your mother wasn't available emotionally, you will probably unconsciously want a wife who is. And if your father never appreciated you, you will want to have a new family experience of being accepted for who you are. Strangely, if you were abused emotionally or physically you will create the same experience with your wife, either by abusing her or by letting her abuse you. As you carry these childhood experiences, you will often unknowingly attempt to rectify unmet childhood needs and emotions in your marriage through interactions with your wife. She, of course, is doing the same thing, and that is the origin of power struggles in marriage.

Each of us has many uncompleted issues, wounds, tendencies, attitudes and hurts from our childhood, no matter how good and kind our parents were. Most of what you think is the essence of "you" is actually a set of feelings and perceptions about yourself and your life formed in childhood from the events and people around you. In addition, you unconsciously took on many of the thinking and feeling patterns of your parents and other family members. Aren't you discovering that you are a lot like your mother in some ways, and your father in others?

Even if you try to create a marriage that is very different from your parents', the internal dynamics will often mirror the behaviors you observed as a child. You can marry a woman who neither looks nor acts like your mother, yet you will unavoidably act out some of the contradictions and conduct of your parents, individually and together. Of course, we may act out many positive patterns as well, which are also learned from our parents. These might include how we play with our children, deal with finances or cooperate to fix dinner.

I learned many positive things from my parents, but much of what I assumed was normal and useful behavior was actually not so workable with my wife. For example, I assumed that because my father stayed so emotionally close to my mother it showed how close they were as a couple. Unfortunately, my wife felt that my "closeness," which I had patterned after my father's, felt suffocating to her. And my father's strong way of upholding standards of right and wrong came off as rigid and demanding. Whether we know it or not, our husband and parenting styles come primarily from our internal experience of our parents. Our learned patterns can get in the way of our ability to fully love our wives, and also block access to our personal joy and power.

In addition to "marrying your parents" to rectify unresolved feelings, you may have unconsciously chosen your wife because she seemed to make up for your own perceived deficiencies in personality, habits or feelings. So, if you are a disorganized, sloppy person, you may have married a woman who is very organized and structured. If you are uncomfortable socially, you may have married an extroverted "people person" to help you out in uncomfortable situations. This is why some people say that we "marry our opposites."

Here is the point: you thought you got married because you were "in love." You thought marriage could satisfy all of your desires—sex, fun, friendship, nurturing and security. What you didn't realize was that you got married because of an unconscious need to heal yourself.

So now what? I hope that you see now how your marriage is partly an attempt to heal your childhood pain. If you can accept this, you can start to learn how to use your marriage to help heal you. I want you to use the multitude of challenges that marriage throws your way as opportunities to notice your childhood hurts and begin to move beyond them. You might not think you can do this, but I'm going to show you how.

Next, we will shine light on one constant challenge we all face: our desires.

YOUR WIFE WON'T SATISFY ALL YOUR DESIRES

We've seen that in the early days of your relationship it felt like your wife held the key to your love and happiness. You weren't the only one who has felt that way. In fact, practically every popular love song of the last hundred years affirms how wonderful life with your loving woman will be. "Night and Day (You Are The One)" by Sinatra, "Only You" by the Platters, "I Need You, I Want You" by Elvis Presley. (Create your own list.) Unfortunately, soon after the wedding it dawns on all of us that our chosen woman can't—or won't—meet a lot of our desires and expectations.

Some desires are simple. Maybe you want someone to stay up with you to watch late night television—but she likes to go to sleep early. Or you like things neat—and she leaves her clothes around. Some are not so simple. You want sex frequently. But she has to be "in the mood." Maybe you want a woman who is great at nurturing her man, but your wife isn't much of an "earth mother." Perhaps you want a slim and sexy woman and your wife is overweight. Whatever the desires, we all eventually learn that our spouses can't always make us feel happy, secure and loved. For most men, this is a constant source of disappointment and conflict in marriage.

No one person, place or thing can satisfy all your desires. Desires are endless—and transitory. A new car is satisfying, but once you get a few scratches on it and own it for a while you want something else to satisfy you. You crave some time alone, but soon want companionship. Every day brings a never-ending stream of desires. Where do all these desires come from? What lies beneath all desires is the yearning to feel satisfied and complete. That is the "desire of all desires"—to feel contented and whole. The less we feel good about ourselves and comfortable with whom we are, the less happy and contented we'll be and the more we'll chase our desires. The more we feel incomplete and miserable, the more we'll find marriage to be a problem and our wives to be insufficient.

Please understand that I'm not telling you that you shouldn't have nice possessions and good friends and family. Many things and people and experiences can be enjoyable and wonderful to have in our lives. Just don't expect any person, place or thing to keep you satisfied and happy every day for the rest of your life because, finally, none of them can satisfy the underlying desire.

DESIRES BEHIND MARRIAGE

We unconsciously expect our wives to satisfy this underlying desire for completeness and love. The reason is because when we were infants and small children most of us had the wonderful feeling that our mothers loved us completely and unconditionally, and that Mom was always there to answer our needs. As adults we have the underlying belief that our wives should love us like our mothers did when we were small. Unfortunately, this belief runs aground and is smashed repeatedly on the sharp rocks of the reality of marriage.

Marriage is not going to be easy and comfortable for most men, no matter how much you want it to be. Hot news flash: marriage to a woman is challenging; women naturally test and challenge men. It's in their DNA to do it. And, as noted, they do it without even trying. I hope you realize that a good marriage in the 21st century is going to trek through unmapped territory—it will have meadows of ease and comfort broken up by frequent, arduous climbs and precipitous falls; every marriage I know of has phases of trial, thunderstorm and difficulty. Life is complicated and messy; appliances break down, kids get sick, bills need to be paid. Don't expect your marriage to be a constant, safe haven from the real world.

I've mentioned the desire to have your wife be like a mother to you. There are other desires that you may never have considered, and they are beneficial. All heterosexual men are, in varying degrees, attracted to women. We think it's because we need them for sex or the biological urge to propagate the species. This is true. We are also drawn to women because we know at some level they can help us bring out our hidden "feminine" qualities—intuition, creativity, fluency with our feelings and increased contact with the spiritual side of life. I also believe that most men have the unconscious desire that their wives will wake them up and help them to become better, more complete people.

This desire—to wake up, to grow in life—can be met through your marriage, if that is what you use it for. You can use your marriage to become a more loving, caring person. I recommend that you put the desire to do this at the top of your list, and that you open up some distance between you and your desires so that they no longer dictate how you live your life and act in your marriage. It's normal to have many desires for your life and your marriage. The question is how you will deal with them.

WORKING WITH YOUR DESIRES IN MARRIAGE

To work with your marriage desires, I want you to learn to distinguish between your true needs and your preferences. True needs are those things you can't get along without, and they are the few "must-haves" you should hold on to in your marriage, so choose them well. Examples of true needs might be: to have your wife pay attention to you and be interested, to spend enough time with you so that you keep up with each other's lives, to have honesty and candor or to have sexual exclusivity. Preferences, on the other hand, are those things you want but can do without if you simply let go of them. Let's say that you really want your wife to cook dinner and have it ready for you after work. Is this an essential need? Or is it a preference—something that you want but can live without? Answer: probably a preference. Or, what if you want your wife to go to baseball games with you but she isn't interested. Preference, or need? Answer: Probably a preference. How about this one: you want your wife to stop focusing so much on your six-month-old baby and at least have sex with you more often. Preference, or need? Answer: for most men, a true need.

OK, let's say that sex with your wife is a true need for you. But your wife is absorbed in caring for your six-month-old baby and isn't at all interested. What do you do? As with any true need, you have to figure out how to get what you truly want. No blame is needed; likewise, no whining. So, you get on the phone and find a babysitter and spend an evening away from home. Don't know any babysitters? Network with others until you find one. If all else fails, work with your wife to plan the babysitter, and use your energy and commitment to make an evening out become a reality. If you really need something, go for it. Your energy and enthusiasm will lift your wife along with you.

When you can mentally file your desires as either "needs" or mere "preferences," you can avoid having them create conflicts between you and your wife, and you can choose your battles well. A while back, I wanted my wife to have the same level of undying commitment to my marriage as I did. I became so adamant about it that it grew to huge proportions in my mind, forcing several confrontations and arguments about how much my wife really "cared" about our marriage. After one frustrating conversation, I finally filed my desire into the "preference" category. I realized I'd still be OK if I didn't have it, and as I let go of it my impatience and anger suddenly lifted. I saw that it was my strong preference that she state her commitment the same way I did, but that it didn't have to be a true need, which I had expressed as an angry demand.

Everybody has desires for marriage. But you will be disappointed if you force the fulfillment of each and every desire upon your wife. When you see yourself becoming disappointed or angry at your wife for not meeting a desire, ask yourself how important the desire really is. Don't get into a heated argument or negotiation unless you are sure that your desire is a "true need" or a "must-have." Unconditional demands have a way of spurring irreconcilable arguments. It's better to state your preferences and give your wife room to discuss them with you.

Marriage requires real work and the ability to honestly look at yourself and change accordingly. You can become another member of the legion of men who divorce their wives and blame them for all their troubles. Or you can use marriage as a vehicle to cultivate a partnership based on mutual support and growth that will benefit you both. One of the keys to the creation of this kind of a marriage is learning how to let go of some of your desires.

Next, we'll look at some tools you can use to take responsibility for your inner growth within your marriage.

CHOOSE TO LEARN FROM YOUR REACTIONS RATHER THAN TO RUN AWAY FROM THEM

Kenny sat on his bed thinking about the argument he just had with his wife, Alison. He stared out the window, so angry he could hardly breathe.

One thought swirled through his mind. He almost said it aloud: "I've had it this time!" He could practically number their arguments, because they were always about the same damned things. Call this latest one "36 B"—the one where she criticizes him for being so preoccupied with work that he doesn't have anything left to give his family.

Kenny stood up and found a clear plastic paperweight on his desk and turned it upside down so that he could see the snow falling on a tiny plastic city inside. White flakes surrounded a tiny car and family near it. He looked away and thought about Alison. Well, if she thought he was so terrible then she could just take the kids and see if she could do better without him! Didn't she see that he was just working hard to give them what they needed? What was so bad about trying to provide for a family? Kenny asked himself.

He flopped on the bed, rolled on his side and took a deep breath. How could he be so well respected at work and such a bum at home? She never saw his good qualities—only the bad. Then a difficult thought came up and just sat there, square in his face. As Kenny looked at it, his heart beat faster and he felt worry, fear and a little panic in the middle of his stomach. Maybe this marriage wasn't working out…maybe he'd be better off on his own…without all the worries and stresses. Should he just call it quits?

Kenny is in full "reaction mode," not thinking clearly about the argument and his reactions to it even though it could reveal important truths to him. He is thinking about running away rather than staying for the real job of learning about himself. What is he missing? First and foremost, he doesn't want to look at his wife's needs or how his focus on work is freezing her and the kids out. At the same time, he's not seeing that his actions are depriving him of a full, loving life. Kenny especially doesn't want to look at his workaholic tendencies and pattern of disappearing into work to hide from his feelings altogether.

Kenny could learn a great deal if he could calm down and look beneath his reactions. But we've all been where Kenny is and we know how hard it can be to get past our feelings. The emotions we feel after an argument obscure what might be causing them, and they sweep us away from rational thought. We all get lost sometimes in our emotional reactions to upsetting circumstances. The question is: What can we do about it? I'm going to show you what you can do, but no matter what I tell you only one thing is really important: what really matters is whether you have the will and the guts to dig into things and learn. It takes a lot to push through strong negative emotions such as anger, sadness, fear or hurt to discover where they come from. You've got to care about yourself—your own growth and clarity and self-knowledge—to go on this voyage. Let's push ahead now and take a look at some tools that can help you on your journey.

PRACTICE THE ART OF SELF-DISCOVERY

We just covered how easy it is to react to situations, and to get stuck in our reaction to them. Let's hear how another man handles the situation with his wife. Here's a couple now....

Ben, a tall, wiry man, and Daisy, a short, red-haired woman, walk in, stage left. Their postures are rigid, their faces tight.

Daisy (moderately): "Honey, why don't you ever take out the trash? I end up doing all the housework even though I have a full-time job just like you. Does that seem fair? I really wish you'd pitch in around here."

Ben (irritated): "Listen, I'm working long hours under a lot of pressure, and I'm pulling in a lot more money than you, so get off my ass! I do a hell of a lot around here and I need some downtime to recover. Why do you continually bitch at me?"

Daisy (walking toward him angrily): "Just put your things away for a start! You throw your clothes and everything else on the floor, or leave them somewhere where I have to pick them up. You're just like a child! Do you think I'm your housekeeper?"

Ben (angry, shouting and walking away): "Just leave me alone! I'm going in the bedroom to have a few minutes to myself for a change. So let's just forget all my stuff. I'll pick it up later if it's so important to you! (Walking away quickly) You feel like you have to control everything around here! I'm really sick of you trying to control me!" (Slams door)

―――――――――――

It looks like Ben has really blown it. I don't know about you, but this sounds pretty familiar to me.

What does Ben think about when he's alone in the bedroom? You've been there, and so have I.

He'll probably spend a good deal of time in internal criticism of his wife and possibly himself. He'll blame her for pushing him too much, and blame himself for being so short-tempered. Either way, he's on the road to frustration, anger and despair. How do you get past the cycle of emotion, blame and criticism once a situation has passed, and go deeper to unearth the truth? Here are four excellent tools that Ben—or you—can use to take another path.

1. Self-inquiry

Self-inquiry is the practice of asking searching questions, and digging until you find the answers. For many people it works best to write down the questions and answers, and to keep a journal of one's discoveries. Otherwise, you can simply contemplate your situation by mentally asking yourself questions. Here are some sample questions you can use:

What am I feeling right now? If your feelings are not clear, ask, What am I thinking about this situation? What's on my mind?

What sensations do I have in my body right now? (Muscle tension, pain in the belly, tense shoulders) What do those body sensations tell me that I feel about the situation?

- What do I want or need in this situation?
- Why do I need it so much?
- What do I expect to get out of this situation?
- What is my part in this situation? How did I help create it?
- What do I need to learn about myself to get a handle on this?
- What can I do differently or better?

You can create your own questions to more clearly reveal the details of your situation. It may take you a little while to calm down enough to start the self-inquiry process. That's OK. As soon as you can collect yourself, take the time to uncover what's causing your reactions. Ben may find out why he reacted the way he did to Daisy's innocuous request to take the trash out, if he would ask himself a few simple questions. He may determine that he's needed more support from her than he's been getting, or that he needs to talk to her about some of the pressures he's been under. He may even remember that he reacted in similar ways to his mother's requests, and that his reaction didn't have much to do with Daisy at all. Self-inquiry is easy, practical and free. I recommend it highly.

2. Kinesiology (otherwise known as "Muscle Testing")

Muscle testing is a great way to practice self-inquiry. I have found it to be the best and fastest way to learn the truth about my reactions, feelings and needs in any situation. I can use it in private and it is easy to use after a little practice. I recommend it without any reservations.

Kinesiology is a science that is taught in many major universities. For our purposes, we'll keep it simple and say that it is the study of your electrical system and muscles. I urge you to be open to it.

Years ago, it was discovered that people's muscles couldn't hold their strength when certain objects or energies were brought into contact with the overall human system. For example, saying, "I'm bad, I'm a bad person" actually causes your muscles to weaken. You may find it extremely helpful to use muscle testing as a way to better understand how you really feel about a situation or person, because your body will tell you the truth about how something is affecting you, even when your mind may be confused.

Most people who learn about kinesiology use it in the following way: You extend one arm and resist someone's pressure on your hand, who is trying to push your arm down. Amazingly, if you put a negative thought, word or object in your "field" (mind or body), you will be unable to keep your arm extended. According to kinesiology, your electrical system is responding to a "negative" by short-circuiting. If you put a positive thought or object in your system, you will easily be able to keep your arm aloft. You will not, of course, always have someone available to help you muscle test whether something is true, or positive for you, so here is a method to muscle test on your own.

(The following directions assume you are right-handed; if you are left-handed, reverse them.) Using your left hand, place the tip of your left thumb on the tip of your left little finger, making a closed electrical circuit. You will use your right hand to test this circuit, so connect the tip of your right thumb and the tip of your right index finger.

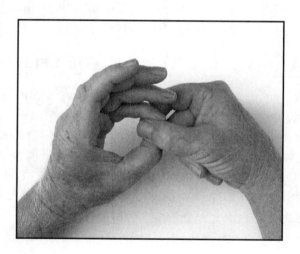

Place your right hand (with the thumb and index finger touching) directly under the left hand's thumb and little finger intersection, and touching them. It should look as if the circuit fingers of the left hand are resting on the test fingers of the right hand. Now you are ready to practice muscle testing.

Keeping this position, make a statement that you already know is either true or false. For example, you might say, "I am married." Or, "I live in the United States of America." As you finish the statement, attempt to pull your left "circuit" fingers apart with your right "test" fingers. Do this by opening the thumb and index fingers of the right hand somewhat forcefully.

If the answer to the question or statement is positive, you will not be able to easily pull apart the (left) circuit fingers, because the electrical circuit will remain intact and your muscles will be strong. Experiment with the amount of pressure in the circuit; you don't need much, just enough to hold it in place. If you want this to work, just relax. Be sure not to try too hard or take it too seriously—just put a circuit together and see if it holds. If the answer is negative, the circuit will pull apart and the electrical circuit is broken. If the answer is positive, the circuit will hold and you will not be able to pull it apart easily.

HOW TO USE MUSCLE TESTING FOR SELF-INQUIRY

Practice with easy, positive and negative answers until you get the hang of muscle testing. Then you can begin to use it to test how you feel about an issue you are contemplating. For example, after another fight with your wife, you might want to discover your part in it and what you need to learn from it. Ben, the man in our example, might think, "I'm angry at Daisy." (The circuit holds, indicating "yes.") "I'm ready to talk it over with her." (The circuit breaks, showing a "no" answer.) "I am sad about this." (The circuit holds.)

Then he thinks, "What am I sad about?" So, he tests, "I'm sad because no matter what I do it feels like it's never enough." (Yes.) Then, he thinks, "Is this about Daisy, or about something in my past?" So he tests, "My sadness and anger are about Daisy." (No.) "This is about my mother—I felt that same sadness about her." (Yes.) Ah-hah! Now Ben has something interesting to explore, and he's learned that his feelings aren't even about his wife at all—they're about his mother!

To make muscle testing work, you need to be somewhat calm and attentive. Too much emotional intensity will throw it off. Ask simple yes/no questions, and don't attempt to have a particular outcome; let the truth reveal itself. If you aren't careful, you can override the true outcome with your emotions and your will, and this will negate the whole experience. Therefore, it's best to get your ego out of it; just relax and see what comes up.

Try muscle testing for at least a few weeks. You'll learn it quickly, and, if you give it a chance, it will become an invaluable discovery tool for you. For example, you could muscle test to determine what emotion you are feeling in a certain work situation, or how you feel about a specific interaction with your wife. You might muscle test whether something your wife accused you of is, in fact, true. Or, you could muscle test whether or not you really want to go to the party on Saturday night that your wife has asked you to attend.

3. Seminars, Workshops, Classes and Groups

You may find it useful to learn more about yourself through group education. Many opportunities abound to learn. You can categorize seminars and workshops as for either the head or the heart, and it's great to sample both types. Education for the head refers to those classes where you learn something intellectually. Education for the heart refers to classes where you learn something that touches you emotionally or spiritually. You may want to take a class or two in communication skills, with or without your wife. (It may touch both the head and the heart.) Or, you could take a class that allows you to use artistic expression as a way to tap into your emotional, intuitive side. (It mainly touches the heart.)

I would recommend that you learn how to meditate. Meditation will help you clear the incessant clutter in your mind, so that you can have a deeper experience of yourself without the layers of your ego and personality. Once you learn how to meditate, you can use meditation daily to calm your mind, acquire more inner peace and strength and move forward in your spiritual development. Of all the things I've learned, meditation has been among the most useful to me.

Over the years, I have taken many classes and seminars and have gained a great deal from various books. I know that you will find the course of study that is best for you. Of course, there are thousands of choices available. The best test of any prospective course of knowledge is whether it brings you closer to knowing yourself.

4. Counseling

A marriage will be smooth or difficult in direct correlation to the mental health of the people in it. To the extent that one or both parties are psychologically troubled the marriage will be difficult. It is a great help to the marriage when each person does whatever he or she can to create mental and emotional health. Contrary to what some people believe, marriage counseling isn't the only answer to a marriage in trouble.

I have had some good experiences with counseling. But not all counselors are effective, and not every situation requires counseling. Don't go to counseling unless you really want it. If you attend only because your wife "makes" you, the counseling probably won't work and you and your wife will both end up angry.

Unfortunately, most marriage counseling doesn't work. Go to marriage counseling only if you and your wife aren't communicating. Marriage counseling can really help open up communication between the two of you, but otherwise it probably won't do much good. Couples who go to marriage counseling in hopes that it will "save" their marriage usually get very disillusioned. On the other hand, you will make the most impact on your marriage and on your entire life if you enthusiastically take part in individual counseling.

Individual counseling works if you sincerely want to understand yourself better. Get a reference from someone you trust and respect, and then check out the counselor. I don't want you to waste money on a "non-directive" counselor—one who just listens. Instead, try to find someone who will work with you in an active way and who can produce results quickly. If you don't have some real progress after a half-dozen sessions, you are most likely with the wrong counselor. Stay open-minded in the sessions and have the bravery to go as deeply as you can into your emotions and thoughts. The counselor is there to guide and help you, but therapy will only be successful if you are one hundred percent signed-on to the work.

As you can tell, there are many avenues to walk along the process of self-discovery. One of the inevitable benefits you will reap from this process is that you will become a more open and vulnerable person. Vulnerability may seem like a weakness but it is actually the opposite. We will explore the topic of vulnerability next.

LEARN TO BE VULNERABLE: IT'S ATTRACTIVE TO YOUR WIFE, AND VITAL FOR YOU

Women always want men to talk, to "open up," and it's often difficult and threatening for us to do so. But when you do, it can melt a woman's heart. Vulnerability is the unguarded expression and acceptance of your inner emotions and thoughts. It's no secret that women find it easier to be vulnerable than men do, because their emotions are closer to the surface and more accessible. Very few men can or should live in the world of vulnerability. However, we can visit that world, enjoy being there and create an emotional connection with the people we love, partly by showing them our vulnerability.

If you want to feel happier and more complete as a person as well as have a healthy marriage, you eventually will want to become more vulnerable. You'll want to be more aware and expressive of your "inner life" of feelings, yearnings, needs and pain. This may seem scary at first. I can tell you from experience that as you begin to focus inward, your life won't fall apart; in fact, it will improve as you become more authentic in your relationships. I used to think that if I opened to my feelings, I would wallow in them and waste a lot of time, becoming useless to myself and others. I also secretly feared that if I felt my feelings I'd never be able to come back to the work-a-day world I wanted to succeed in. What I discovered is that becoming aware of my feelings slowed me down a little, but once I felt my feelings they would clear and I would have more energy available to me. Best of all, when I clear the feelings out of the way I feel more like myself than ever.

You may think it's "unproductive" to show vulnerability in your work-life, and that may be true depending on how you make your living. In many situations in life, it's inappropriate to show your vulnerability. If someone at lunch asks you to pass the salt and you begin to cry, it might be a problem! However, the real problem occurs when you bring your work-a-day, "armored" demeanor home. If you are like the majority of men, you feel most energized and confident at work, and, frequently, your attention is necessarily directed outward toward performance. That's natural. However, intimate relationships require more intimate communication and less "performance"; that's what makes them deeper and more fulfilling than casual relationships. You will only create trouble for yourself and your wife if you face an intimate situation with a closed and "productive" approach.

VULNERABILITY AND SHAME

When you are vulnerable, you may be surprised by the strong feelings of shame you feel for not performing or having it together. We want so badly to perform well and "look good" at all times. According to some psychologists, shame is our first defense against feelings of vulnerability. We experience vulnerability as being "out of control," feminine or weak, and if we drop our guard a little we can feel ashamed by what we show—tears, weakness and hurt. When you feel uncomfortable or embarrassed by what you reveal, shame is probably underneath.

One of the ways a married man handles feelings of shame is to project the shame onto his wife. We may criticize our wives' appearance, housework, cooking, language, intellect, etc., rather than experience the shame ourselves. If we can make our wives "bad," then we can feel better. Obviously, this is something you want to be on the lookout for and avoid doing. You can stop doing this if you are willing to look at your own feelings about being vulnerable. Now, I want to ask you a question: when did you shut down and begin to guard against your own vulnerability?

GROWING UP MEANS LOSING VULNERABILITY [GROWING UP MEANS PUTTING ON ARMOR]

If you are like most men, as a small boy you were dependent on adults, particularly your mother and other women. And like most boys under the age of five or six, you felt vulnerable at times and were somewhat sensitive. In a way, you were easily "feminine"—that is, you could be sensitive, emotional, hurt, lonely, weak and vulnerable to others close to you. You expressed your feelings easily to the women around you, and didn't feel there was anything wrong with it.

Then at the age of six or seven, and on into adolescence, you learned you weren't supposed to cry or show signs of weakness. You were told by kids on the playground to stop being a sissy or a girl, and to "be a man." Maybe your father, or other adults, told you the same thing. Ever since, as with almost all boys, you learned to cover up your "feminine" feelings of vulnerability and stuff them down when they surfaced around others who could hurt you. But don't you sometimes long for your early childhood, for the time when you didn't have the burden of being super-masculine and always-strong? There are times when you just want to drop the responsibility of having to "perform," carry the load and be on guard.

In this way, men are full of ambivalence about vulnerability. We long for it, but we fear it as well.

PRACTICE VULNERABILITY— OPEN UP THE LINES OF COMMUNICATION

You can plan for and practice vulnerability, even in work situations, but it is most effective when practiced in the moment as part of your everyday interactions. You do this by tuning in to your own inner "barometer." "How do I feel?" "What do I really want/need?" "What is my truth here?" Ask questions to delve deeply and prompt more authentic interactions with your co-workers and family. Take a risk: feel and express your own truth about things.

When you find yourself censoring your own speech with your wife or others ("She won't like that." "It will just start a fight. I'd better not say that.") you are resisting vulnerability and keeping up appearances simply to perform. Although this is natural for a man, it is a dangerous habit that needs to be broken.

You can learn to name your feelings and to be honest about your needs. You can learn to talk about what you feel inside (without relying on an internal censor) and speak in a way that respects others. If you can't express what's inside, talk about that with someone you trust—preferably your wife or a counselor. Talk about your work, your boss, your co-workers. Talk about your frustrations, hopes, needs and past. Talk about your life.

If you want a loving marriage, you would do well to drop as much as you can of the unconscious patterns and feelings that are in the way of your authentic self. Vulnerability is the necessary vehicle to get on the road to that destination. Some men find it helpful to work with a counselor over a period of time before they feel comfortable being vulnerable, even with (or especially with) their wife. If you are locked into angry positions of criticism and attack with your wife, it's understandable that you would want to feel safe before you leave yourself open. A critical woman can damage a man's attempt to be vulnerable. Women have no idea how easily they can shame a man, particularly when he is open. Being vulnerable and open runs counter to what men do naturally. If a woman attacks, we may shut down even more and create new defensive armor.

Nevertheless, if you really want to feel close to your wife, as well as to yourself, learn how to be vulnerable and authentic about your true feelings and thoughts.

VULNERABILITY MAKES YOU MORE POWERFUL AND FLEXIBLE

Look, men in ages past had good reason to armor themselves when they needed to fight real enemies—animal or human. Those days are long past, yet we still instinctively close down our feelings and create a suit of mental and emotional armor to battle the world. Perhaps you think this makes you powerful. Paradoxically— because you have more of your natural, real self available—you are far more powerful and strong when you know where you stand emotionally.

Wearing a suit of heavy armor takes immense energy. Shoving down your emotions steals energy and will eventually shrivel and weaken you. Not least, it's tough to make a marriage successful if we are constantly protected and on guard with our loved ones.

Vulnerability implies swift strength, awareness and letting go. It is pure flexibility—the ability to move appropriately and lightly with whatever the situation requires. Vulnerability is authentic and real, and there is power in that. When you are vulnerable, you are closer to your real self and don't need to constantly perform for others.

Actually it's a relief to quit pretending and just let go. When the façade is gone, we can be so much more joyful and playful with others. All the energy we use to protect ourselves will then become available to create the life we choose.

I have come to admire men who have the guts to be open and honest about their feelings and needs. They have more of themselves available to give to relationships and they have more satisfaction in life. I know men in their sixties, seventies and older who have shut down. They have refused to deal with their inner pain for so long that they seem cut off from themselves and others around them. Depression and resignation with life sets in. It's painful to be around men like this. Their marriages are empty, and often it seems they are just waiting to die.

Closing yourself off from your emotions and pain may at first seem the easy way out. But take a look around and you will see a great many men who are bottled-up inside. They are hurting inside but lying about it outside; merely keeping a false persona in place to "protect" themselves. Even though this seems easy, even natural, men suffer tremendously for this kind of effort to keep things together. The older you get, the more you will suffer in your effort to hold your armor in place.

Have the guts to drop the shields you are holding. You won't be unprotected because you don't need the protection in the first place. Your path to freedom and power is to find safe forums that allow you to drop the false personas you adopt. Be courageous. Start now.

You'll need to be vulnerable if you want intimacy with your wife. I know you can do it. Please go farther with me as we look closely at intimacy in marriage.

BECOME COMFORTABLE WITH INTIMACY
AND IT WILL PAY OFF IN YOUR MARRIAGE

What is intimacy? Webster's dictionary defines intimacy as "a close, familiar and usually affectionate or loving relationship with another person." How do you create intimacy in marriage? It is created through vulnerable, honest, authentic verbal and non-verbal communication between husband and wife. Note: intimacy does not necessarily involve sexual intercourse, although men usually want it to end up there!

When you communicate intimately, you are able to speak openly about your deepest feelings and hear another's feelings with compassion and without passing judgment. You are able to reveal your hurts and fears, and to compassionately hear another's hurts and fears. You are willing to be honest, to cry and to show a full range of emotions. Most importantly, you are willing to do all of this in front of someone you love dearly, a person who can probably bring out your worst reactions and defenses.

For men, being intimate can seem as if it were a loss of some kind, a sacrifice of control to a woman. This is scary. It brings up issues of trust and elicits childhood fears of being revealed as weak and ridiculed as "being a baby." Just to be able to open up and show our "weaker" side to anyone is to overcome our feelings of shame and inadequacy and our fears of being destroyed by women in our life. But facing this fear is well worth it.

Men are often surprised that intimate communication can bring them closer to their wives. They may be even more surprised to discover that intimacy brings them closer to themselves. Women know this intuitively; men have to learn it. If you've ever wondered why you "have to" talk about your feelings when you are with your wife, it's because she wants to feel close to you and she knows that open, intimate communication brings you together.

You don't always need to talk to be intimate with your wife. Affectionate, warm touching does the trick, too. Women many times seem to enjoy being intimate this way more than through having sex. It may take practice, but you can have sex without intimacy quite easily. Yet at some point you will find—if you haven't already—that intimacy adds an incredible dimension to the sexual experience. The way to make sexuality more intimate is to change your objective about sex to "connecting" instead of "coming." To finding instead of merely releasing. As you open yourself to your partner, you will find that you can stay in the moment more easily and just enjoy touching.

This will require that you open up to a subtle interchange of signals between your wife and you—eye contact, kissing, touching and, most of all, taking enough time to learn what gives her pleasure. Given a choice, women would almost always rather have sex that is founded on intimacy, although many women today are "learning to think like men" and enjoy sex on its own terms. Regardless, almost every woman wants verbal and/or non-verbal intimacy before sex. Intimacy prepares the way for them.

Over time, in the proper settings, you will find that you will enjoy intimate communication of all types because it is more authentic and opens you to a deeper experience of yourself. Sometimes it can be a relief to let go of the armored covering you keep around yourself. Intimacy will draw you and your wife closer together, and help you grow as a person. It will bring more love into your life.

One more thing: true intimacy starts from within you; it's not a technique. As you learn to become comfortable and knowledgeable about your intimate inner life, you can share it more easily with your wife. Otherwise, intimacy becomes a parlor trick. Your wife says, "Talk to me about your feelings. Let's share." And you have nothing to share. Women may think men can share their feelings on command. I don't know about you, but when I hear this kind of demand I naturally resent it and resist opening up. I don't want to be a trained dog; I want to open up when and how I want to. And, I want the option of not opening up, too. When you do the inner work to become intimate with yourself, you can talk or not talk; it's your choice and you have the power over it.

I'll tell you quite a bit about how to communicate with your wife in the next step, so please read on and investigate the third major step, "Tune In to Your Wife."

CHAPTER FOUR

Step Three: Tune In to Your Wife

FIND OUT WHAT SHE LIKES AND NEEDS

Women quite often say that their husbands don't understand them, that they don't really see them. This chapter intends to show you how to tune in to your wife and communicate and relate to her so that your marriage works for both of you.

In general, your wife needs three things from you. She needs you to:

- Listen to her, absorb what she is saying and feeling and respect what she says
- Treat her as a full equal and give her your respect and love
- Stay awake and engaged in your life and in your marriage

If you concentrate on fulfilling these three tasks, you'll most likely do fine in your marriage. However, this step, "tuning in" to your wife, is pretty challenging. The key to tuning in to your wife is to be curious, and to genuinely care about her world. This can be a chore. First of all, as many men see it, women seem to talk so much! Sometimes it gets tiresome to listen. Second, much of her world just isn't that interesting to you. If it were, you'd probably be a woman, not a man. Somehow, women have the capacity to understand their men. They may not understand what's going on in your job, or why you love sports or something else so much, but you can bet they know a hell of a lot more about you than you do about them.

It's curious that the average wife knows so much about her husband and he knows so little about her. A woman typically takes an interest in her husband and provides physical, emotional and spiritual support to him, and does it (usually) in a giving manner. Most men, on the other hand, can rarely be bothered to understand their wives or take much interest in their activities. Why?

We men are usually interested in action and performance—who wins and who loses in sports and politics. We watch the game on TV, read the newspaper, concentrate on work issues, finish projects, work on the computer, etc. We love the challenge of competition, and crave the chance to be a hero. If we can't be a hero, we like to watch other heroes engage in battle through sports, politics, business or war.

Women are usually more adept at relationships. They tune in to the worlds of feelings, empathy, support to friends and family, connection and harmony. Even ambitious businesswomen usually handle relationships well while they work their way to the top. Watch the women's cable channels (WE, Lifetime, etc.) and you will learn what women are attracted to: stories about love, women in danger and complicated relationships of all kinds.

LEARNING ABOUT YOUR WIFE

There's no point in trying to become more like your wife. In fact, I strongly recommend against it. However, you can set out to understand her likes and needs better. Why would you want to do that? It will accomplish two results:

First, you will be a more engaged, understanding and caring husband, which will make your marriage easier and better.

Second, when you open your mind and heart to your wife more, it brings you more joy. This is one of the fundamental principles of life on Earth: care about another person, open up to her, and you'll feel more love. Marriage provides a relatively safe venue to do this, at deeper and deeper levels.

If you can appreciate another person and fully accept her flaws, needs and imperfections you will be uplifted. Marriage is a path to grow close to another person—so close that you eventually see her as no different from yourself. Ultimately this means that you see her essence, her very being or consciousness. Amazingly, you learn it is the same as your own.

But let's start simply along the path to learn more and tune in to your wife. Over time, spend a few minutes watching, learning and listening. Ask questions and pay attention. Think of it as a laboratory experiment; it can be fascinating to see how different your woman is from you, how she thinks and feels about her life. Here is a list of some of the basic things that you can discover about your wife and some advice about how to approach each.

Clothes—You don't have to know much to see whether she likes loose clothes or tight, up-to-date or vintage, upscale or bargain basement. Look at colors, collars, sweaters and tops. Women are remarkably aware of all these things. Even sophisticated, intelligent women want to stay in fashion and spend time combing through magazines to stay current. I wouldn't recommend buying clothes for your wife unless you love to take risks. I stopped buying clothes for my wife early in our marriage after I bought the wrong size, color and style dress. Other than those reservations, she loved it.

Jewelry—Almost all women love jewelry and, given enough money, would buy tons of it. If you want to buy her jewelry as a present, earrings are easy to understand and to buy; bracelets and necklaces are more difficult, but not impossible. Notice whether she goes for silver or gold, flashy or subdued, large or small earrings. Stay away from buying rings unless she is with you; they're tricky.

Colors—It's useful to know her favorites, and with a little practice you can begin to see which colors look best on her, bring out her eyes, skin tone, etc. No, I'm not kidding! The only caveat here is to keep your color and fashion advice to yourself unless she asks for it—and then, tread carefully.

Shoes—Are you kidding? Don't even try to get into the world of women's shoes unless you are willing to quit your job and study this subject for a few solid months.

Foods—Some women love it if you order for them at a restaurant; most don't. You can buy her favorite foods at the grocery store and cook if you dare.

Flowers—It is useful to know if she likes a few special types of flowers. You can buy them for special occasions, or simply appreciate them with her as you see them around town. Don't automatically assume that buying your wife flowers is a great idea and will please her. The advertising industry has put forth the lie that all women like chocolates or flowers or greeting cards. Find out for yourself.

Touching—This is absolutely essential to know. You may be surprised at what you can learn by asking. Ask about back-scratching, preferred massage touch, affectionate stroking and sensitive (sensual) areas.

Kissing—An important essential. You can go for years without learning what kind of kissing she likes the best. This fact is amazing to most guys, but most women won't tell you unless you ask and really want to know.

Worries—Sure, you hear a lot of them, but what are the big ones, the ones you don't know about, the ones she is keeping to herself? You don't have to solve the worries or make them better. Just listen. Yeah, I know this isn't so easy sometimes, especially when your wife wants to "process" with you when a game or some other favorite show is on TV.

Sex—This is probably the biggest one of all. You definitely need to know what she likes, and she probably hasn't told you if you haven't asked. You will need to set up an atmosphere of safety and loving acceptance to find out her likes and dislikes. Talk about sex when you are feeling secure and a little playful—make it easy and fun to talk about it. You should also be willing to genuinely learn and accept whatever she says. If she can't or won't tell you, let her know that it's OK to show you what she likes, without talking, during intercourse. She can move your hands and your bodies around as she sees fit. I encourage you to discuss and/or watch and learn about this. Good sex can get you through a lot of hard times.

Hopes and Dreams—Encourage and support whatever you hear, no matter how impractical her hopes and dreams seem. Avoid imposing logic or specific plans on her hopes and dreams. I've crushed more than a few of my wife's dreams by telling her, without meaning to, that her schemes won't work. Again, just listen and appreciate and love her. She'll love it that you are on her side and know what's in her heart.

As you know, women are still learning how to deal with their new opportunities and choices in society. As they expand into the workforce, politics and other areas previously off-limits to them, it can present many challenges for men. I'd like to tell you a bit about women, power and equality in the next few pages.

TREATING YOUR WIFE AS AN EQUAL MAKES HER MORE INTERESTING AND CREATES MORE LOVE

During the course of history men have generally had it easy in marriage, at least compared to women. The history of marriage in America and the rest of the world is partly a history of the subjugation of women. Women have been treated as second-class citizens in their role as a wife until very recently in the West, and they continue being second-class in large areas around the world. Have you ever wondered why young men traditionally asked the father for his daughter's hand in marriage? The custom indicates respect, but it's also because fathers have always "given away" their daughters because they were little more than property and the patriarch controlled his daughter's choices.

For thousands of years, brides and their fathers were expected to contribute a dowry of property and money to a marriage, and wives were not allowed to own property because they were seen as people who needed to be taken care of. The law has traditionally been much tougher on women who had extramarital affairs than on men, primarily because women were supposed to be chaste and because the man's status was threatened by the "rebellion" of his wife's sexual affair.

It is likely not a coincidence that women became more interesting to men when they began to enjoy equal opportunities and social power. It's hard to feel romantic about someone you believe is beneath you. Interestingly, the romantic ballads of the 12th century European troubadours were directed at women of a high social order, women who were out of reach. These songs were all about longing for the unattainable—powerful queens, princesses and noble-women. In the 20th century, women gradually became more equal to men in society, and as they did their power and attraction and allure increased.

Many men feel romantically and sexually attracted to, as well as threatened by, powerful women. Maybe we want to conquer them as we compete with them. Perhaps power is sexy. Regardless of the reason, it is to our advantage to help women be powerful in our society, and to help your wife be powerful as well. As a woman feels her power, she becomes less reliant on a man to take care of her. For men, this can feel like a huge rejection and the loss of a prized role in life.

A man named Jeff loved being the breadwinner and sole support of his family. He felt good about his job as an IT professional and the salary that came with it. When his children reached their teenage years, his wife, Belinda, joined the workforce. Soon, she landed a great job as a salesperson and started to bring in huge amounts of money, much more than Jeff. At first, Jeff told everyone how proud he was of his wife and how glad he was to have the extra money. Soon, he became tired of cooking dinners when she was late. He began to resent how tired she was in the evenings, and how much she out-earned him. Most of all, he resented her new friends and her social nights out with them. He began to feel left out and unneeded. For the first time in his life, he felt like a house-husband and loser.

Jeff suffered in silence for a while, and then he broke down and talked to Belinda. Almost in tears, he told her how he felt and how much he missed her just being his wife. And then a funny thing happened. As they talked it over, he began to see how much Belinda had changed for the better. He saw that she was more self-confident and she looked better. He realized that she was considerably more interesting and sexy than in the past, and that he was more excited to be around her. Most important, he realized that he needed to be glad for her and work with his own feelings of rejection. In short, he learned that he needed to get over it. In those few minutes, Jeff made the decision to step up to the plate and let his wife be powerful in whatever way she needed, and to match her power with his own. He resolved to overcome the logistics of the situation and meet the challenge of a smart, powerful wife. At the same time, he began to ask for what he needed from her and to negotiate from a position of power, rather than weakness. In the weeks that followed, he was able to get more of her time and attention and she was pleased with his new stance. One more thing happened: their sex life improved a lot.

It is also true that some women do not want to be equal with their men, or are conflicted about it. They want to take advantage of the new roles society is providing for women but they don't want to give up their own femininity and the roles in the home that have made them happy. For example, many women are having a hard time juggling motherhood and their careers. If your wife is ambivalent about advancing her own power and growth through a new career, or is attracted but scared to break out of an old, limiting role, I have a suggestion for you. Support your wife's advancement and growth. I don't want you to ever stand in her way of expansion, for two reasons. First, you will be blamed as the impediment: "I could have done so much if you would have let me!" Second, it is to your benefit to be with a woman who is moving ahead in whatever direction she chooses. She may be more challenging to live with, and life will be less safe and predictable, but your relationship will be more alive and the sex will be better if you both are powerfully moving ahead in life. And, women who have a sense of direction and purpose feel better about themselves and are far easier to be with.

You already know that much of marriage isn't always fun and romance and sex. It's hard work and conflict and growth. But a large part of marriage is just being together—shopping, talking, watching TV, cooking dinner and more. All things being equal, your chances to stay together for a lifetime improve greatly if you are great friends and companions. Friendship is our next topic.

FRIENDSHIP WILL HELP KEEP YOU TOGETHER

Do you have an old, close friend, someone you've known for many years? You can go several months or years without talking, and when you do speak you pick up as though nothing has changed. He could have gone through many changes, but whatever he has done it really doesn't matter—because he is your friend anyway and you forgive him and care about him regardless.

This is friendship: loving, trusting, forgiving and loyal. If you can create a great friendship with your wife, you will love and forgive her through almost anything, and survive the rough waters ahead. Besides, you will have a companion—a teammate—through life to play with. If you are not friends, you can be separated much more easily because blame and criticism and resentment will creep into your relationship. If you aren't friends, you will complain about your wife to others in a way you never would about a close friend.

You can become better friends with your wife the same way you would with anybody:

- Treat her with respect and courtesy
- Listen to her with interest
- Plan activities and spend some fun time together; hang out and enjoy each other
- Open up about yourself and share what you're going through
- Say positive things to her every day, and forgive most of her negative traits

If you genuinely can't see your wife as a friend and partner, your chances of staying together for the long haul are slim. If you want a life companion you should start with the basics of friendship: acceptance and forgiveness and good communication. Romance and excitement may fade, but friendship and partnership will last.

YOUR JOB IS TO PROMOTE YOUR WIFE'S WELL-BEING

Try this scenario: Your wife hasn't seen her eighty-two-year-old father in several years, because she has a number of resentments about his lack of attention and harsh nature. The father doesn't care for you, and you don't much care for him, either. One day you overhear her taking a phone call from him.

"No, Dad! It just won't work. I'm sorry," she says, as she hangs up the phone.

"Who was that?" you ask.

"No one."

You have trouble believing what you've just heard. You think for a minute and say, "Wasn't that your father?"

"Yeah, it was."

"And..."

"And, he wanted to come and visit but I said, 'Absolutely not.'

We've just got too much going on and I can't handle the stress."

———————

What would you do in this situation?

One option would be to let her decide for herself—she's a big girl and it's her life, not yours. So you'd say:

"OK, honey, whatever you think is best...."

However, if you are committed to "promoting your wife's well-being," you would go another route. The rest of the conversation might go like this:

"That doesn't sound like a good idea. First of all, your father is getting on in years and he's not going to live forever. Not only that, but you haven't resolved your issues with him...and you need to, I think."

"But, I don't want to see him. Besides, I've already told him 'No.'"

"What if I called him? Let me talk to him and see what happens."

"OK, I guess so, but I'm scared."

"I'll call him and tell him we want him here. I know he doesn't like me much, but I know he loves you and wants to see you."

———————

This is a true story. The man who shared it with me called his wife's father, who lived in Europe. The father agreed to come if his daughter called and invited him. She called, and he came. The husband stayed away much of the visit and cared for their small children, while the wife and her father spent time together talking.

The father's visit lasted a week, and he died just a few months later. The wife's sisters were terribly upset because they had "unfinished business" with their father, while the wife felt incredibly glad that she had worked out her relationship issues and was now at peace.

TOO MUCH EMOTIONAL INVOLVEMENT RENDERS YOU UNABLE TO HELP YOUR WIFE

It takes courage and commitment to be this kind of husband. You have to be able to see, dispassionately, what would be best for your wife, then take whatever actions are necessary for her well-being. What you can't do is to get emotionally involved in the situation.

What if the husband in the preceding example had let his fear of involvement enter into the situation? "You're right; your dad doesn't like either one of us! He's a mean old S.O.B. The hell with him!"

With this course of action, the father dies having not visited his daughter, and the daughter carries guilt and bad feelings with her for years. She suffers with it and you suffer with her.

Your wife has relationships with her friends, clients or others, and she has many dilemmas in her life. The trick is to not get sucked into her "story" about them, or involve your feelings on her behalf. Instead, you must stay separate and unbiased enough to see what's best for her, and act on that information in a compassionate yet unemotional way.

What if you can't see what is best for her? Listen with empathy, and refrain from giving advice until you can clearly see the truth of the situation. Love your wife and see the best in her, and usually the truth of the situation will make itself clear.

One of the main things that separates the men from the boys when it comes to marriage is the ability to stand up and challenge your wife to move ahead, or to stand with her against an enemy. Earlier, I mentioned that women are very good at challenging their men. For men, it's usually a learned skill. But it can and should be learned. You learn this by making a commitment to your wife and to the quality of your relationship. Sometimes, you have to stand up with her and against her fears or weaknesses, even if she is buying into them. Sometimes, you have to stand up with her against actual enemies, like a serious illness or injury. A friend of mine cared for his wife, who had cancer, for five years until her death. He did it with diligence and love, and he rarely complained. Once I asked him how he'd been able to do it for all those years, and he said, "Because I told her I would stay with her all the way until the end."

Now we're ready to get into the nuts and bolts of communication. Let's start with how to listen.

IF YOU WANT IT TO WORK, LEARN TO LISTEN

Wife: (Thinking, "We don't go out much anymore. We need to spend more time together and feel close to each other again.")

"Do you want to go out tonight?"

Husband: (Thinking he has been asked a factual question)

"No, not really."

Wife: (Feeling hurt that he doesn't care enough to be with her)

"Really?"

Husband: (Irritated and wondering why she is asking him again)

"Yes, I just said I don't want to."

Wife: (Showing her hurt now) "OK, if you don't want to...."

Husband: (Mystified) "Is something wrong?"

Wife: "No, we'll just stay home, I guess...."

Husband: "OK, whatever...." (He goes back to his newspaper.)

Most men are naturally more focused on outward action than inward introspection. Thousands of years of evolution have trained us to hunt, protect, work or pursue. When ancient men had to fight a human or animal enemy, I'm sure they didn't hone their abilities to be in touch with their feelings.

Over eons, men developed the ability to complete tasks well and communicate about their work. Task-oriented, analytical communication is very useful and appropriate in many situations, especially at work. This kind of communication requires the ability to produce and perform—to "go out and kill"—by isolating facts, asking tough, specific questions and generating quick, useful solutions to spontaneous problems.

Men are less skilled at the style of communication that builds and maintains relationships. This type of communication utilizes empathy, feelings and intuition, and requires the ability to read the message beyond the literal words. In the interchange above between the man and woman, the woman's questions ("Do you want to go out tonight?" "Really?") communicate much more than her words. You need to cultivate a higher level of attention and skill to hear what's behind your wife's "simple" questions and offhand remarks. Communication like this is literally "communion with" another person.

We men are good at hearing the literal meaning of our wives' messages, and good at solving the problems they present, even if our mates don't want them solved. We are not as good at reading their non-verbal messages, including tone of voice, facial expressions, eye contact and body posture. In other words, we are good at facts and solutions but we have more trouble with feelings and subtle meanings.

If women naturally want to connect, feel emotions and discuss things out-loud, it is natural that your wife would also want you to listen and interact with her in order to feel close to you. Listening—really listening—is for your benefit, too. If you can listen fully, it will open you up to compassion and caring, and you will find it easier to acknowledge your own emotions as well as your wife's.

You need not be afraid of emotions—hers or yours. They are just feelings; they come and go and only acquire power over you when you ignore them. But make the time to listen, and listen with your whole heart. Feel her emotions the best you can, understand her needs and don't solve any problems until she asks for advice. Just listen. Don't talk or try to be smart. You don't have to listen like a woman, with some great sense of female intuition; you merely have to listen like a human being.

I taught listening skills for many, many years before I learned something basic. When you listen to women you usually don't need to say a word! I used to try at home lots of the fancy stuff that I taught people in my management seminars. It not only fell flat but my wife usually blew her top when I tried it. I learned the hard way that what she really wanted was simply my undivided, heartfelt attention. She could tell when I was tuned in and when I wasn't. She didn't need me to summarize or comment or anything else. She just wanted me to hear her.

When you listen, stay away from advice unless she asks you for it. Giving advice or feedback without being asked will usually be perceived as trying to take control, and all too often it will backfire on you. You may feel that you understand the issue and have some good answers for her. Other men might appreciate your interjections, but your wife will not. She would rather that you listen empathetically. If she wants your advice, she'll let you know. If you have to give advice, respectfully seek permission first.

TWO KINDS OF LISTENING

There are two kinds of listening: analytical/problem-solving listening and open listening.

Analytical/problem-solving listening is the type most men are proficient at. This approach to listening attempts to break a problem down into component parts through questions so that it can be rapidly solved. "Did you try to call Henry about that?" "Why did that happen?" "Why didn't you do that?" "Let me tell you what I think you could try."

These questions are useful to collect information essential in problem solving. Most work situations require this kind of listening, and most males prefer it. It assumes a free exchange of data and advice and a rapid exchange of potential ideas and answers. When two men get together, they usually use this type of listening, even for serious emotional problems.

First Man: "My wife left me last week."

Second Man: "Bummer! When did she leave?"

First Man: "On Wednesday."

Second Man: "Jeez. Where are you going to live?"

First Man: "I don't know."

Second Man: "I thought you two were doing OK."

First Man: "I thought so, too."

Second Man: "Didn't you two go to a counselor?"

First Man: "Yeah."

Second Man: "Well, the whole thing sucks. Maybe we should go out for a beer."

This kind of listening is composed of mostly "closed questions," which require only a short answer and factual, unemotional responses. It may work for men together sometimes, but it is not a good fit for serious, emotional conversations with a woman. We can get into huge trouble if we stay in the analytical/problem-solving mode when the situation requires what I call "open listening." Believe me, your wife will find it objectionable and demeaning to have to be on the witness stand for cross-examination as you fire questions at her to hurry the conversation along. She is looking for open listening and basic understanding and feeling, which don't come easily to most men.

When you practice open listening, you hear the issue, problem or data in such a way that the other person feels truly heard or acknowledged and validated. Your listening may result in a collaborative exchange of options to solve a problem—but only after you have fully heard the entire message, including the facts and her thoughts, opinions, feelings and needs. Open listening is the type of listening that is most needed in a marriage, especially in these circumstances:

- An emotionally-driven situation where your wife needs help or assistance to solve a problem. ("Honey, I don't know what I'm going to do. I have so much on my plate right now I don't think I'll ever get it done. I'm so stressed out!")
- Emotionally-charged conflicts. ("You don't pull your weight with the kids. They need a father around here. I can't be their father and mother both!")
- A serious exchange of intimate, revealing information. ("I feel so inadequate to do it. I'm just a big loser. I don't think I've ever been good at much of anything. I put up a good front with everybody but I'm scared I can't measure up to their expectations.")

To be in the "open listening" mode you must focus on feelings more than facts and allow plenty of time for your wife to talk. You have to learn to listen on two tracks, collecting the basic content but also taking in the "context." You might think of it as listening to both the words and the music of the song. At the same time that you are collecting the data (i.e., what happened, when, to whom, why, etc.), you also observe and feel what she is feeling. One thing that most men (and many women, too) do is to listen too urgently. They want to dig in, understand and fix the problem immediately. Again, in "open listening" situations, this is a mistake. Instead, take your time. Take your cues from your wife for when/if she wants solutions.

ASKING QUESTIONS

It may be useful to ask a few questions, and "open questions" are usually best. Open questions require the speaker to talk more. Here are some examples of words to use in open questions:

"What are your thoughts about what happened?"

"How do you see your choices in this situation?"

"Tell me about what happened…"

"Help me understand how you feel about this."

Just acquire information and let her talk freely. In general, stay away from the word "why" ("Why do you feel that way?"), because it asks her to explain or justify her point of view, and it will just make her angry. Again, for many situations you are better off just listening without saying a word. With practice, you'll learn when to ask questions and when to stay silent.

EMPATHY AND EMOTION

Here is an important general rule about listening:

The more emotional she is, the more you need to listen with empathy and the less you need to talk.

Of course empathy doesn't always have to be verbal. Sometimes you can show empathy simply by showing concern or matching her facial expressions. To show empathy, start by putting all of your attention on her. Don't let your mind wander or try to jump ahead to the answer to her problems. Very quietly, let yourself feel some of what she is feeling. Just "be" with her for a while. You will want to keep enough distance in the conversation so that you can be helpful; drop your emotional guard. Here is the time to become vulnerable and humble; this is no time for ego. If you are unable to understand what she is feeling, don't worry about it. It will probably be revealed in time. The most important thing is that you tune in to your wife and show you are listening as deeply as you can.

If you want to respond verbally to her feelings, you can offer identification statements or empathy statements. Identification statements come about when you can put yourself in her shoes and identify with her situation. An example might be, "I've had that happen to me and it's really hard to take." Be careful that you don't tell your own story when you offer identification statements, as in, "You know, that reminds me of when I faced that once at work. What happened was...."

Empathy statements focus on the other person's feelings or situation. They might include: "I know that's difficult for you. That really hurts." "You must feel awful about that." "You really got hit hard today." If you are unsure what your wife is feeling, you'd best not say anything. Just listen with great attention, caring and compassion.

One more technique that might help is what some call "summary statements." Summary statements can be useful to make sure that you have heard correctly, and they also let the speaker know that you have been paying attention. Summarizing her response lets her hear her situation or problem back in a neutral way. Some examples are: "So, what you are saying is...." Or, "Let me see if I understand. You are saying that...(and summarize the issue)." Or, "The issue is...."

If you summarize bits of her message, remember to do it accurately, simply and without any of your own "spin." Please remember that the higher her emotions are the less you will want to summarize back the content. In very emotional conversations, summarizing may even make your wife angry, because it just gets in the way. In those cases, just be quiet and attentive and, if you can, show empathy either non-verbally or verbally.

LISTEN WITH RESPECT AND TAKE ACTION

Ultimately there is only one thing that matters when you listen to your wife: to listen to her with love and respect. A compassionate witness doesn't need to talk much—or at all. He truly "gets" what his wife is communicating, and he really sees her in a way that perhaps no one else does.

In our culture, so many women feel invalidated, discarded, even damaged by their parents and the expectations and demands that society puts upon them. So many women have issues with self-esteem and body image in a way that few of us understand. If you can only be there and listen to who your mate is and what she goes through you will become her invaluable friend and compassionate lover.

Listening is the most important communication skill you can have in a marriage or, for that matter, in any relationship. The next most important skill is the ability to speak your mind in a respectful, coherent way. You'll learn more about speaking in the next section.

SPEAK YOUR OWN TRUTH

One thing that's easy to do in a marriage is complain.

"Damn, why don't we ever have clean clothes around here?" "The house is a mess!" "I need a little space. Can't you keep the kids quiet so I can relax for a few minutes?" "Work is such a drag. I don't know if I can stand another day of it!"

Recreational complaining may serve a purpose at times, but complaining can tear down a relationship, and it certainly doesn't build good communication. On the other hand, many men believe that they are better off simply saying, "Yes, dear" to pacify their wives, stuffing their real feelings because they want to avoid conflict at home.

If you have a turbulent work life, you can be excused for wanting a peaceful home front. However, you can't achieve peace at home by being passive and accommodating. When you do, you are sending your wife a message that you don't care and that she can do whatever she wants. This only makes her frustrated because she doesn't have a partner with whom to interact. No one can have a genuine relationship with a rag doll that won't push back or speak up.

Frequent complaints and the "Yes, dear" syndrome are ways of hiding your real thoughts and feelings. The more you hide what you really think and feel, the more you are cheating your marriage out of the lifeblood it needs to thrive. Close relationships need honest communication and revealing exchanges from both parties. Your fear of conflict or laziness is not a good excuse for holding back. You can say, "I don't really care. I just want to be left alone." But that's not enough to feed a marriage, or act as a man with integrity and purpose. If you want to pull your weight in your marriage you must learn to speak up, however awkward your attempts may seem.

Many men are so cut off from their feelings that they genuinely don't know what they feel or even what they need. All they know is what they think. If you are one of these men, you may be getting by with a super-analytical approach to life and relationships, one that gives you very little genuine joy and depth. To turn this around, you will have to want to find out why you are so cut off from your feelings.

Please be aware that until you can access and talk reasonably well about your inner "truths," you will never have a rich experience in life and marriage. Ask for help from your wife, a friend or a counselor. Or simply start to tune in and ask yourself, "What do I really want in this situation?" or "What am I feeling?... What sensations do I feel in my body?... What is going on with me?" You may never be able to talk about your feelings the way a woman might—that is not the goal. But you can be an authentic person who is working to understand his feelings and reactions to life and to voice them as well as he can. Men sometimes do best by showing what we feel. We're action-oriented creatures. The problem occurs when your wife can't decipher what you are demonstrating (or trying not to demonstrate). Not all women are terrific mind readers. Today, more and more women demand that their husbands learn how to verbalize some of what they feel. I can tell you from experience that it feels better to talk about it than to have your woman guess about it. Every time I'm bottled up and can't, or won't, talk, it makes my wife madder than before. She goes nuts if I don't speak up. So, start to talk about what's going on inside. You will not be perfect; that's OK. You are learning, so cut yourself some slack.

Speaking your mind gives you strength. In doing so, you express your own internal truths and shape your own environment and relationships accordingly. This way, life doesn't just happen to you. You possess real integrity because you are able to talk forthrightly and sincerely, and you can be "real" with your wife and other people, too.

I was in a business meeting recently with a corporate client, and the group was about to go in a direction that I knew wouldn't be effective. Their ideas would also make my work harder later on. In the past, I probably wouldn't have troubled to speak up. I always figured that I'd clean up the mess later and I didn't want to risk not being liked. This time, I spoke up. I pointed out the benefits of another direction and shaped the conversation that way. I got what I wanted, and no one seemed the least bit concerned that I'd spoken up; in fact, they seemed impressed with my expertise. Later on, I realized that my habit of speaking up with my wife transferred neatly to business.

HOW TO SAY WHAT YOU MEAN— AND NOT CAUSE TROUBLE

Communication isn't female or male, it's neutral, and anyone can do it. First, let's break down some categories of speech communication.

FACTS

You can speak about facts when you want to start a conversation or keep it calm. Facts are indisputably true and agreed upon. A fact is, "We have been married for ten years." Or, "Last night we went to the movies." When you speak about facts, you will automatically be speaking from a position of agreement (you both know it's true), and you will not incite conflict.

The problem comes when you state something as if it were a fact when it is not. You might say, "Last night you dragged me to the movies!" This statement is a judgment, or conclusion, about the fact that you went to the movies together. Most men speak about facts quite easily, and use logic as if it were a sword. I want you to learn to use facts and logic consciously, as a way to set in motion a deeper exchange. If you rely on the more simple factual approach too much you will be moving against the grain of what marriage requires.

JUDGMENTS AND CONCLUSIONS

Your judgments or conclusions are your perceptions or beliefs about what is true, as opposed to those facts that are recognized as true by everybody. Whenever you use judgments or conclusions about others, you run a high risk of creating anger and disagreement because they are perceived as attacks. Suppose you say: "You're just not trying to hear my side of this!" "I don't think you even have a clue what I mean!" These are your judgments but they may not have any basis in truth. Even if true, the words may sound hurtful and attacking. If your wife doesn't share the same judgment, she may react very negatively. I have learned that most of my judgments are too harsh and unforgiving, and I'm working on communicating them less.

On the other hand, you can profitably speak about your judgments, opinions or conclusions if you claim them as your own. You might say, "This is my perception...but I believe that...." or, "I may be wrong, but it seems to me that...." This way, your judgments don't masquerade as the truth—you're just presenting what is in your mind and what seems to be true.

You may find that it's better to express your judgments as your needs. For example, rather than saying, "I don't think you even care about me or how I feel!" you might say, "I need to know you understand me, and for you to show me that you care about me."

Stay away from words such as "always" and "never," since they seem attacking and they close off the possibility of something being true "occasionally," "sometimes" or "frequently." Besides, "always" and "never" are rarely true. If you say, "You never let me speak!" the truth is that your wife probably let you speak at least once or twice during the past several years. Or, if you say, "You interrupt me each time I begin a story!" she probably let you finish a story at least once or twice during the past few years. Instead, you might say, "It seems to me that you often interrupt me when I tell a story...."

Here is one tip about presenting any "bad news": wait until the emotions have cooled a little. The more inflamed your emotions are the more your wife will read the music, regardless of what your words say. Also, using the words "it seems to me" or "my perception is" takes some of the sting out of your judgment or criticism. It presents what could sound like an attack as a more tentative judgment.

FEELINGS

Emotions are by nature irrational, or seemingly beyond reason. You don't have to explain them or justify them—just realize you have them. Men may have a hard time naming a specific feeling; we just know we feel bad or good. You may want to work with someone—a friend (yes, even your wife!) or a therapist—to help you identify and name specific feelings. You can also utilize kinesiology (muscle testing), which can help you to identify a specific feeling before you talk about it. (You can review pages 102 through 105 for information on kinesiology.)

To talk about a feeling, remember a feeling is just one word that describes an emotional response. Thus: *sad, dejected, lonely, frustrated, pissed off, disappointed, panicky, scared, worried, nervous, elated, thrilled, glad, peaceful* and *contented* are just a few of hundreds of words that express feelings.

One way to determine if you are describing a feeling is to notice if you use the word "that." When you do, you are not describing a feeling at all. For example, you might say, "I feel that you aren't as committed as I am to teaching the kids about money." This statement is a judgment, a belief or a thought—but not a feeling. Similarly, "I just feel that you aren't trying very hard" is a judgment (which sounds accusatory). It is not a feeling.

A feeling statement might be, "I feel frustrated (a feeling) because it seems to me that you aren't as committed as I am (a judgment or conclusion) to teaching the kids about money." Another is, "I feel worried (a feeling) that we aren't ready (a judgment or conclusion) for the big gathering over here this weekend."

If you can't name an emotion precisely, use general feeling words, such as "sad," "angry," "afraid," "worried" or "concerned." If you have trouble stating any feeling at all, it's OK. If you practice, it will get easier. Meanwhile, just talk as best you can about the hurt or pain or joy or whatever is true for you. Sometimes, the best you can do is to say, "I feel bad (or good) because…." Try to take responsibility for your side of the communication, and avoid using words that put the blame on your wife. Very soon, your sincere effort will pay off in good communication, and in better relations.

NEEDS

Your needs are among the most important things you can learn to express to your wife. Earlier, we looked at dividing some of your needs into "preferences." Whether they are preferences or needs, you still have to talk about them in the right way. The more you are aware of your needs and can articulate them without blaming or criticizing, the happier you and your wife will be. Your wife may not know what you need or want, and until she does you have no chance of getting your needs met. Even if she can't grant your needs, just your stating them aloud will improve your relationship since marriage is inevitably about understanding and adjusting to the other's needs. The more clearly you say what you want, the more your wife will understand you. You'll have hard, clear edges instead of fuzzy, wimpy ones.

One tip is to share only one need at a time. "I'd like to go out for a camping trip with my buddies three weekends from now." Declare only those needs that your wife has a reasonable chance to do something about now or in the near future. For example, if you say, "Don't ever talk to me when I'm trying to get my work done!" she will probably balk at agreeing to that request because it's too difficult (don't "ever" talk to you?). On the other hand, if you say, "Hey, this work is really important. Can I ask you to interrupt me only if it's urgent—if you really feel it's urgent?" Then she may find it an easier request to accept.

PUTTING IT ALL TOGETHER

I don't expect you to rehearse what you are going to say to your wife every time you speak. What I'd like you to do is occasionally think, "What do I want to say?"—and do that before you open your mouth, especially during difficult conversations. Once you understand some categories of expression, you can pick and choose from among them. Remember, women respond very well to expressions of feelings; so if you can learn to express some basic feelings—"I feel angry," "I'm sad," "I feel happy about...."—you will get your wife's attention quickly. In the same way, she will respond positively to your responsible expression of needs, as long as you give her plenty of room to have her own reactions. And remember, be careful in your use of judgments or conclusions (e.g., "You just don't care about me!"). Such expressions are likely to cause strong, angry responses unless you couch them carefully, as in, "It seems to me that...." or,

"My perception is…." or, "From my perspective…."

Alternatively, it's fine to talk in a "stream of consciousness" style, so long as you are tuning in to your inner world. Don't worry if it's not perfect. The more you are able to express yourself responsibly, the more proficient at communication you will become and the more satisfied you and your loved ones will be.

And remember, listening is more important than speaking. No matter how artfully you bring up a subject, it will often explode in your face if you don't listen well to your wife's reactions. That's why we need to look now at the subject of defensiveness—your own and your wife's.

YOUR DEFENSIVENESS DECREASES YOUR POWER AND INCREASES HER CRITICISM

Getting defensive is natural, but it's something to avoid as much as you can because of its destructive effects. When you get defensive, all of your energy goes into defending yourself; none is left for constructive communication. Even worse, defensiveness escalates every situation it touches and increases the fire of anger in your mate. Finally, the more defensive you are the weaker you become and the more out of control and less able you are to speak and hear the truth.

What is defensiveness? It is an emotional reaction to something that challenges your sense of self-esteem or your sense of "being OK." A typical stimulus could be your wife's feedback or criticism of your values, behavior, work, habits or family. For example, "You never seem to care about the kids," "Why can't you pay more attention to me instead of the TV?" "You talk too much about yourself and you're not listening to me at all." Once you identify yourself with the object of the criticism, it's easy to see it as a threat to your value as a human being. When you feel threatened, you naturally want to protect yourself and will respond in defensive ways.

THE D-J-A—DENY, JUSTIFY, ATTACK—RESPONSE

One typical defensive reaction is sulky, passive-aggressive behavior such as physically showing anger and hurt while verbally saying, "I'm fine, I don't care at all." This is a passive-aggression reaction. The words are positive, but the music is negative. When you see yourself or others giving this kind of "double level" message, know that you are dealing with defensiveness. By far the most common defensive reaction is what I call "D-J-A"—Deny, Justify, Attack.

Let's hear how the D-J-A reaction sounds. For example, your wife says, "I work full-time just cleaning up your messes around here. You must think I'm your slave!" Your D-J-A defensive reaction might sound like this: Deny—"That's just not true and you know it!" Justify—"I try my best around here and work like a dog for this family." Attack—"And you constantly criticize and complain about everything I do!" If you watch closely, you'll soon see a lot of D-J-A reactions in daily life. Many teenagers have a special talent for this.

The worst thing about a D-J-A reaction is that it almost always generates a response of the same kind: another D-J-A. So your wife might respond with, (D) "I don't criticize you half as much as I could. (J) I take so much from you without ever saying a word. (A) But you are impossibly lazy about helping out around here."

You can see how your defensive reaction can produce something similar in your partner, and thus create escalation of the argument. Begin to see your own defensiveness. Pay attention to what brings it up at work and at home. Don't judge it. Just watch how it makes you feel and what it creates in your interactions with others. Trace it back to your initial reactions to what others said or did, and see whether you felt somehow diminished or "not OK." Remember, we get defensive when we believe that we have to protect ourselves.

The next time you get defensive, observe your emotional responses. They might include anger, passive-aggressiveness, sulking, manipulative behaviors and hurt feelings. After a while, you will short-circuit your defensive reactions. You'll begin to pull back from defensiveness soon after you see it flash forward. You'll see that defensiveness only makes you weaker and inflames every situation it touches. You may never eliminate all signs of defensiveness, but, in time, it will no longer dominate you or your marriage.

What can you do when your wife is defensive? The first thing I'd recommend is to see her emotional reaction as defensiveness. If you do, you can pull back and think, "Oh, she's being defensive! She's protecting herself because she thinks I'm attacking her." You might see the D-J-A, pouting, passive-aggressiveness or other emotional reactions. Once you name her reactions (mentally) as defensiveness, that's your signal to stop talking.

The key to defusing defensiveness is to disarm your wife's defenses by refusing to attack. Instead of taking the bait (responding to her D-J-A or other defensive behaviors), become quiet and shift your focus to "listener mode." Be compassionate. Think of her defensive reactions as natural; she feels wounded and somehow lessened. Your job, then, is to simply listen and acknowledge her defense. Notice how she's feeling. Her angry reaction isn't as important as the fact that she feels wounded. Ask questions, summarize and empathize if you wish. But remember what I mentioned in the previous section on listening: sometimes, it's best to just keep quiet and show you care.

We'll continue our focus on communicating with your wife in our next section. We're going to tackle one of the biggest problems most guys face in their marriage: the incessant criticism they get from their wives. Please read on.

IF YOUR WIFE IS AGGRESSIVE TOWARD YOU, STAND YOUR GROUND AND LISTEN— UP TO A POINT

"Why do wives complain and criticize so much?" Well, one reason is they think you aren't listening to their complaints and criticisms—as very possibly you're not—so they think they need to speak louder and more insistently. They continue the "beatings" because they think you still don't "get it"! Another reason is that women who root out the truth (at least the truth as they see it) in a loved one are exercising their feminine power. Criticism or the desire to change a man is as natural to them as swimming is to a fish; it's just what they do, at least until you learn how to take your power back.

I know one man who long ago "tuned out" his wife's criticism. His wife rants and raves but she is sort of "de-fanged"; she knows her criticism is falling on deaf ears and she seems defeated. Her husband sits there, seemingly unperturbed, never saying a word. Eventually her complaints run down and she becomes silent. This pattern repeats itself day after day. In fact, it appears to be one of the central pillars of their marriage. How miserable they both seem: locked into self-defeating behaviors that long ago doused the dwindling spark in their marriage. It seems obvious that their approach to criticism doesn't feed either individual, or the marriage as a whole. Yet, like many marriage partners, they continue, stuck on "permanent depress" cycle.

I know another man who fights back when he hears his wife's criticism. Their house is full of acrimony and mutual recriminations. You can feel the tension within the four walls of their house. He never gives an inch and neither does she. What a marriage; "The Bickersons," I call them.

Criticism can range from mild suggestions to insistent nagging. Sometimes a woman's criticism will turn into aggressive, nasty attacks. If you haven't seen this fiery aspect of women, count yourself as lucky. Nothing seems to work when a woman gets this wound up. If you lower your head and take the fire, your wife may lose respect for you and become even more angry. If, on the other hand, you fight back you can fan the fire into a blaze that might eventually destroy the trust and respect that holds up your marriage. So how should you react to this kind of aggressiveness?

First, let's remember that your true purpose of marriage is to grow as a person—for you to become strong and loving as a man. Therefore, you must find your masculine power—detached, immovable, knowledgeable and secure in its own nature. From that stance, you can stand firm and attempt to determine if the aggression is based on your improper, or inadequate, behavior. If it is you can extract the elements of truth from her attack, learn what you can and entertain the possibility of changing. Re-state what the "charge" is against you, reflect on it and if you aren't ready to speak about it, say, "OK, I need to look at this some more. Thank you for shining a light on it." There's no need to defend, although there may be a need to apologize. Whatever you do, make it clear that you are in charge of your inner growth. You appreciate the feedback and you acknowledge the help; but you don't lower your head for more beatings!

If the attack has gotten out of control, become quiet and strong. Speak softly, if at all, and keep your focus inside, not on your wife. Monitor your own reactions and do your best to stay centered. Try not to feel superior or judgmental about how wound up she seems; that will just make things worse. Remember that you love the woman no matter how crazy she seems. There's no point in arguing with your wife by using logic when she is that upset; her emotions are too high and you will only make things worse.

Whether the criticism is merited or not, avoid making excuses to defend or mounting a counter-attack. After a while if you find that your wife's aggression is too much to take, feel very free to retreat until she changes her tone. You will know to leave if the criticism becomes abusive, violent or cruel. To shout and attack is one thing. To hurl vicious insults is another. You don't need to be abused by anybody, including your wife; respect yourself too much for that. Sometimes, the best way to handle out-of-control criticism is simply to walk away.

I want you to look at criticism from another angle. This time we'll see how you can turn it into a man's strength: the accomplishment of specific tasks. We'll cover that in the next section.

CRITICISMS ARE OFTEN REQUESTS IN DISGUISE

As I mentioned in the previous section, the reason your wife keeps repeating the same criticism of you is that she thinks you aren't really listening. So listen. But I want you to listen to criticisms in a different way. Instead of getting defensive and providing excuses, use all your power to hear the core of the criticism.

Therapist and author John Welwood says that if you listen and ask questions about any criticism, you will find that there is usually a hidden request within it. A request involves something your wife needs you to change or do better. A request could range from "put away your clothes" to "stop interrupting" to "I want to go dancing and have some fun." If we take Welwood's advice, we can listen for the hidden request.

Here are some examples of how criticism can contain hidden requests:

Wife: "The yard is starting to look like a jungle. Why can't you spend a little time doing some yard work?"

The hidden request: (This is an easy one) "Please do some yard work."

Wife: "You spend so much time watching sports on TV that you practically live on that couch!"

The hidden request: (Another easy one) "Please spend more time being available to me and the family."

Wife: "You seem tired and frustrated all the time and I don't know why. You seem angry but you never talk about what's going on."

The hidden request: (A little more difficult) "I really need us to connect more. I want to feel closer to you and understand how you feel. I'm concerned about you."

Wife: "Your diet is terrible. You have to start eating better and stop drinking so much beer."

The hidden request: (An easy one) "Please take a look at your food and drink habits because I'm worried about you. Can you talk to me about it and let me help a little?"

Wife: "Every time I try to tell you something is important to me, you start trying to tell me what to do. Do you think you have all the answers? You are so focused on yourself!"

The hidden request: (A little more difficult) "Please just listen to me and show me that you care about me. I need you to pay attention and connect with me, not to solve my problems."

Men usually do better when we have specific tasks we can master. Do your best to turn general criticisms into specific requests, which become specific actions you can take to make the marriage work. The obvious benefit is that you will have more harmony in your marriage. The hidden benefit is that you will most likely become a better person as you shine a light on aspects of your personality and internal makeup that have been hidden from you over the years.

We've looked at defensiveness and criticism. Now, it's time to take on major arguments and conflicts.

HAVE THE GUTS TO STAY AND FIGHT— BUT FIGHT WITH INTEGRITY

Every marriage contains conflict. If it doesn't, something is definitely wrong with the marriage. Conflict is a natural part of life. People inevitably have differences. The differences may be about:

- Goals: family budgets, savings, home buying, vacations
- Roles: what husbands, wives and children "should" be like
- Values: one spouse places a lot of value on family togetherness, while the other values fun, parties and entertainment
- Needs: one spouse needs a lot of alone time, and the other needs plentiful time with friends

Think about some of your recent conflicts and you can probably place them in one or more of the above categories. Whatever the cause of any conflict, the way you handle it will reflect your past conditioning and experiences—especially how your family dealt with conflicts when you were a child.

Jerry, 43, had a father who was explosive and frequently lost his temper and shouted at his wife and children. His older brother was also volatile, so these two males frequently fought in the home while Jerry and his mother tried (unsuccessfully) to make peace. Jerry learned early in life that conflict was messy and upsetting and to be avoided at all costs.

In marriage, Jerry shied away from conflict. When his wife, Ginger, attempted to bring up an explosive issue, he walked away or changed the subject. He assumed that things would get better and that nothing was worth arguing over. Jerry was a master at the classic conciliatory strategy—"Yes, honey, you are probably right about that. I agree!"

Jerry thinks this is a useful approach to conflict, and sometimes he's correct. He avoids many useless arguments that way. On the other hand, he is creating some major problems: his wife is losing respect for him because he never stands up strongly for himself. Jerry's passive, backing-down approach has indicated to his wife that she is in control, that he doesn't care enough to fight and that she can have her way. This is dispiriting for Ginger because she desperately wants an involved, engaged husband.

Jerry is also losing respect for himself, although he may not know it. He has lost touch with his own desires and zeal for life, in a futile attempt to keep "trouble" out of his marriage. This kind of marriage has no passion, no friction and no fire. Unless he changes his method of dealing with conflict, Jerry will lose his wife one way or another.

A thirty-seven-year-old marketing manager named Darren acted differently in his marital conflicts. Darren avoided many arguments because he knew himself very well. When he was a boy, his family argued at the dinner table, in the family room and in the car. Whoever shouted the loudest usually won the argument. Darren believed now that only one person could win every conflict—and it might as well be him. He saw every conflict as a win-lose situation. Darren was quite good at arguing with his wife, Dina, and with his colleagues at work. He always knew where he stood on every issue and what he wanted out of every disagreement.

Competitive by nature, Darren listened for the holes in Dina's arguments and then attacked her points one by one. In fact, he relished his marital conflicts, although he had learned that he'd better choose his arguments; Dina eventually cried and gave up when he knocked down her point of view.

Darren's approach to conflict was beginning to make his wife resent him. He was intimidating and overbearing. His loud talk and interruptions didn't leave enough room for Dina, and she was becoming angry that he didn't care enough to listen to her and look for a way for them to work things out together. She was tired of the effort and the stress, and she was tired of the battles.

Darren's competitive approach to conflict and Jerry's accommodating one have something in common: each approach will wear down a marriage. If you want a healthy marriage, you must have healthy conflict. Your own emotional, out-of-control feelings that arise during marital arguments will be the biggest barrier to your ability to fight with integrity. You can influence and often determine the course of an argument by your own conduct, so the key to conflict resolution is to increase your awareness of your patterns around conflict so that you can change them.

Now, let me tell you about Gene and his wife, Pat. They have their fights, just like most couples. Gene handles his side of them a little differently than most, though, and that has made a big difference in their marriage. Gene was raised by parents who refused to fight in front of their children. When the tension increased between them they would retreat to their bedroom to argue. As a boy, Gene would sometimes listen outside his parents' bedroom door as they yelled at each other. It upset him greatly and confused him as well, because he sensed a disparity between the serene image his parents presented and what went on in private.

When he married Pat, they had a child within a year. Gene tried to keep everything under control during their arguments. "Quiet, the baby will hear!" he would whisper. "Let's keep our voices down." He was horrified to find that asking her to calm down just made her angrier. After some time, Gene began to notice that he really didn't feel as calm as he tried to sound. In fact, he was really angry during most of their arguments, and he eventually began to act it out by slamming doors, yelling and throwing things around the room. All this only escalated their conflicts further and exhausted him.

One day, Gene tried a different approach. He and Pat were discussing their money situation, specifically, how little they had and what to do about it. He could feel the tension in the room rising. Gene was about to go on the attack as usual. What he did instead was to talk to his wife. He told Pat how much he wanted to create a good home for her and the baby, and how sad and defeated he felt by their money troubles. He also told her that he wanted to be united with her and on the same side of the fence. He was surprised that his heartfelt speech didn't make much difference.

Pat reacted with tears and anger and strode around the room. She said she felt blamed for their money problems, when she was just trying to set up a good home for them. "Why don't you help me set up a budget? Why are you always criticizing my spending? Do you think it's easy to take care of this baby and also hold down a part-time job?" she cried.

Gene just listened for a while. Then he told her he could tell how hurt she was by his accusations, and how much he appreciated what she was doing to create a nice home. He let her talk some more and kept listening, sometimes interjecting his own side of things but this time without blaming her for his difficulties. After a while, the steam went out of the conversation. Things got quieter. "What should we do? There's got to be a few things we haven't tried," he said. At that point, the dialogue changed. They generated several ideas and gradually a plan took shape to change some of their behavior around money. At the end of their talk, he and Pat were affectionate and loving. It was as if they had climbed a big hill and gotten to the other side.

That one argument changed their marriage. Their arguments didn't stop; they just got less damaging. Things were said, they opened up the bucket of emotions and then they moved on.

MANAGING CONFLICT

We can learn a great deal from the story of Gene and Pat. Think about the quarrels you have had with your wife that ended successfully. (You may have to remember a long way back!) You will notice that there is a point in every successful conflict when one of you begins to listen to the other, even if only slightly. At that point, the air begins to go out of the conflict balloon.

Without trying, the tension subsides, the decibel level lowers and you both lighten up some. "Yes, you have a point. I guess I have been doing that a little...." The moment you are able to drop your passionate "defend and attack" strategy, you can listen with genuine curiosity and care. And that will almost automatically cause your wife to tone down her own "attack and defend" behavior.

Fighting with integrity means that after the initial volleys are fired, you drop your position on the issues and listen to understand and accept her message. You don't walk away, and you don't try to "win." You don't make personal attacks (i.e., "If you'd stop being such a bitch we could get somewhere!"). Instead, you state your point of view as truly and sincerely as you can—and take ownership of it. That's what Gene did in the story above.

Tell your wife what's going on inside you, and don't hold back. ("I am so damned frustrated I can't stand it. It seems like we are getting nowhere. I just want to make this work.") Listen to her point of view, feelings, needs and perceptions, even if you don't agree with them. Remember, empathy is most important when emotions are high; therefore, demonstrate verbal and non-verbal empathy. ("OK, I can see why you'd be angry because you can't get any time by yourself to do what you want.") Care enough to see where the conflict takes you. In other words, don't presuppose that you have the "right" answer. Be willing to see what options arise out of the conversation, and what you can learn about yourself. You have to hang in there with an open mind and see what happens. Believe it or not, most conflicts can turn into collaborative discussions if you stay with them long enough.

Here is what I recommend you do when conflict comes up:

Step 1-Conflict begins: Stay in the room regardless of what happens, and do your best to persuade her not to leave either.

Step 2-Conflict heats up: Speak up, but refrain from throwing personal attacks. Don't ambush her motives, values, personality or family. If she becomes abusive, violent or cruel and you can't take it, this is the time to leave the room. If you are the one who becomes abusive, stop immediately and apologize. If things have gone too far to save, go in the other room to cool off and apologize again later. Then, learn your lesson and never abuse your wife in a physical, mental or emotional way.

Step 3-Turn to listening: As soon as you can, drop your attack and listen to her point of view, to learn and better understand what is setting her off.

Step 4-Your turn: State your own point of view, sticking to how you feel and what you need. (Remember: no attacks!)

Step 5-Be open to solutions: Open the door and let multiple options arise. Don't be in a hurry to solve the problem; it will only inflame the situation. Keep talking until you reach a resolution. If it's absolutely impossible to resolve things at one sitting, agree with your wife that you will re-visit the issue. Then do it. A little time will usually give you both a fresh perspective.

Remember, conflict can be healthy and it helps you and your wife clear away the old, dead brush so that something fresh and new can grow in your marriage. Lead the way through marital conflict with your own integrity. We'll look at one more point about conflict and criticism now: the "Key Moment."

WATCH FOR THE "KEY MOMENT"
AND TURN THE CONFLICT AROUND

Phil and Paula had been arguing for twenty minutes. The volume and negative feelings were on the rise, and they had begun to hurl accusations and long-held hurts at each other.

Paula: "You haven't gone with me to see my mother in years! And you always come up with an excuse why she can't come and visit!"

Phil: "I've been busy, and every time you want to go see her it's during a busy time at work. You may not understand it, but my work is what gives you the new dress you're wearing. I can't just leave work anytime you want!"

Paula: "If you cared enough you'd make time for my family. You wanted to marry me, but I can't cut off my family from my life. I love them! Are you asking me to choose?"

Phil: "No, of course not! You need to keep good relations with your family; we both know that. Just go see them without me!"

Paula locked eyes with Phil and pointed her finger: "The truth is you've always looked down on my family! You think you're better than they are! You've never accepted them!"

Phil was taken aback. He paused, visibly shaken, then sat down on a high-backed chair. This time he was really angry. But way back, somewhere around the edges of his mind, he wondered if what she said was true.

In almost every bit of strong criticism or conflict, there is a moment when your wife turns her ire onto you and says something so cutting, yet so true, that you can't stand it. That's the moment of truth: Do you stand firm and take the information in, or do you deflect it and fight back?

In the example above, Phil must make that choice. If he is smart, he'll gauge the truth of this information in his open heart before he says a word.

There is a saying that goes, "What you resist tends to persist." In other words, pushing against something (or somebody) just makes them push back that much harder. You can shove down any recurrent feelings you want, but they will rise again in your physical body, thoughts or emotions until you are finally willing to let them bubble to the surface and feel them and face them.

Similarly, uncomfortable truths about yourself can be avoided or ignored, for as long as you like—but do so at your own peril. If you refuse to face the issues that your wife brings up, you will make her much more angry and frustrated. Worse still, you will miss a huge opportunity to face things that need to be faced and you'll set yourself up for more pain in the future.

This is not meant to imply that everything your wife says about you is true. She, like others, may make unfair judgments and accusations. On the other hand, she knows you well—probably better than anybody else. If you give her the benefit of the doubt, you can learn a lot. Besides, you are the ultimate judge of whether something said about you is true. If you're brutally honest with yourself, you will usually know in the private space of your heart whether something is true or not.

The bigger issue is that you must first want to know the truth about yourself. No one wants to be hurt or criticized or judged, especially by someone you love and trust. However, if you can't take criticism from your wife you are probably not ready to have an adult relationship based on trust, openness and growth. You may believe that she isn't ready to have that kind of relationship, either, and you may be right.

In that case, you have to set the tone of the relationship and lead her by your readiness to take tough, honest feedback about yourself. That will show her you care about her enough to really listen to and value her comments, and that you care enough about yourself to fully take in and evaluate her criticisms. If you do this, you may be amazed at what happens to your arguments: They become ways to break through old barriers, deepen your relationship and accelerate your own growth. Every marriage has conflict—or should. Don't be afraid of fighting and don't try to win every time, either. Use arguments to bring out the truth of a situation and to move you to new insights. If you do this, it will help your marriage stay alive. You won't be stuck in old patterns of disagreement that you just cover over and that stay there simmering under the surface. My advice to you is to face conflicts head-on. Listen deeply to your wife. And let the truth come out.

The next section looks at partnership around the house. I have some recommendations that I think will help you stay out of trouble, so please read on.

PULL YOUR OWN WEIGHT

As I've mentioned, for many years the marriage equation has been "the man provides and the woman takes care of the family." Most of us men would love for this balance of roles to still apply. If it did, you'd be pampered when you got home, king of the castle. How many men live that way today? I sure don't. The trouble is, your wife is almost always on duty at home, and, if she's like many women today, she resents having to pull all the weight. With a few simple changes, you can avoid this ongoing quarrel and create more harmony at home.

You probably don't know it, but your wife feels responsible for keeping track of the entire household. She's aware of family emotional issues you've never even considered. If she's like most women, she keeps track of schedules, child care, laundry and food, and when something's lost she knows where to find it. Very few men understand the extent to which women monitor and manage a household, and even fewer see the stressful toll it takes on women to hold everything together, whether they are employed outside the home or not.

When a working woman returns home she, in effect, takes on another job as her husband relaxes or plays with the children. You may have gotten somewhat of a free ride this way, but it really isn't free because your wife will eventually burst with resentment and anger. Because they do so much, women often complain that men don't pull their weight at home. If she doesn't complain to you, she probably says it to her friends—or to her therapist. Men, of course, complain that women want too much done, have impossibly high standards and criticize too much.

I want you to break up this logjam. It blocks energy that could be freed up for your relationship to flourish. Here's what I want you to do. Let your wife do what she's good at—managing much of the household—and let her manage your household participation, too. Now, before you react to that, let me explain. I don't want you to work for your wife. What I want you to do is step up your participation around the home and to negotiate exactly what new tasks you'll do.

To take on more around the home you will have to step up your energy and commitment to your wife and the functioning of your home. If you think of your marriage as a full partnership, it makes more sense to do this. And remember: you will do this partly to help her but also to help you become more alive, energetic and committed to your marriage.

Start by seeing, really seeing, all of the things your spouse does, and acknowledge her contribution. I'll bet she does much more than you realize. Ask her to request some things you could do that would help take some of the pressure and responsibility off her. Feel free to suggest a few tasks that you feel comfortable with and to reject others, but don't be afraid to take on tasks that you've never considered. It's remarkable that some household tasks are labeled as "men's work" and some seen as suitable only for women. Taking out the trash is men's work; dusting is for women. Barbecuing on Sunday is men's work; cooking during the week is for women. Where did we get these distinctions? When friends come to visit, who makes the guest bed for them? I'll bet it's your wife. I'm not advocating a total upheaval of your household. I'm only saying that you can take on more than you've done previously, and it would be appreciated and move things your way.

Whatever you commit to doing, master it; make it your own. Do your best in whatever tasks you take on. And if your wife wants them done "better" (loading the dishwasher comes to mind here), let her jump in to correct the task as needed. But don't take her perfectionism personally; you will be fulfilling your end of the bargain, and, if she wants to improve the tasks you've done, stay open to her approach but not intimidated by it.

I also want you to go the extra mile and communicate where you are and when you'll be home. Husbands who neglect to call home to tell their spouses they will be late, deserve the hard time their wives give them. Always keep in touch regarding your schedule and your individual and joint plans; cell phones have made this a snap. When in doubt, communicate. You will rarely be criticized for over-communicating. And, once again, you will be pulling your weight in the marriage. If you pull your weight, you'll live with a more contented woman and you'll help create a more joyful marriage.

And now it's time to talk about sex. Let's start with a fundamental difference between men and women.

MEN HAVE SEX TO CONNECT— WOMEN WANT TO CONNECT BEFORE HAVING SEX

It is true that sex is a union between two people, and that every good marriage is about union. However, true union is union with something greater than the ego, something greater than your limited self. Sex can only occasionally offer that kind of union, and if you put too much importance on it you will get way off track. But sex is important to most men and to most marriages. It can bring you and your wife closer together or much farther apart. It depends on how you approach it. Unfortunately, we live in an age when we are deluged with what is written and said about sex, and little of what's said is worth anything.

Here's a fundamental fact: men and women have different needs when they approach sex. Many men think of sex as fundamentally simple. You insert "Tab A" into "Slot B" and you continue until done. What women often want is much more subtle. They want connection with their man through intimacy. They want to experience honest and deep communication. They desire sensual touching. Holding and caressing with an open heart. Romance. After intimate connection, they will feel more comfortable, loved and open, and they'll usually more readily welcome sex.

It's not that women don't sometimes just want good sex, because sometimes a woman can be sexually open—even aggressive. It's just that in the long run, you will have more and better sex, as well as more loving feelings, if you will create a general atmosphere of intimacy and trust in your marriage and you remember to connect with your wife.

SOMETIMES YOU WANT SEX JUST FOR SEX; OTHER TIMES...

Why do you want sex? If you're like most men, you have sex to:

- Get a release from work or other pressures
- Avoid dealing with emotions you don't understand
- Feel close to, or nurtured by, a woman you love and trust
- Feel powerful or in control

- Act out aggression
- Feel less alone
- Celebrate something great
- Get over something terrible
- Connect in a basic, primary way with your wife

Very often, sex isn't just sex; we use sex to express our deepest emotions, frustrations, and joys. There is no great harm in this. The harm comes when you act unconsciously and are insensitive to the feelings and needs of your wife. This can push her away, when you really want to draw her closer.

If your wife says that you seek to have "too much" sex, she may be sensing that the sex isn't so much about her as about you. If this is the case, spend some time looking at your needs and feelings, and you may see that sex may not always be the answer to your emotional needs.

When you push to have sex out of your own unconscious needs, you will probably not draw your wife into the activity as much. She may be going through the motions to please you, and you may feel a lot less fulfilled than when you have sex that fully engages you both.

It takes time to understand your unconscious sexual needs. Begin to notice how often sex comes up when you are feeling insecure, unhappy or emotional. When you find that you want sex for reasons other than "just sex," examine your unconscious needs before you try to resolve them through sex. Look at the need and see whether it's best dealt with through intimate conversation, private reflection, physical exercise—or good sex.

It's OK to have sex for all sorts of reasons. It's also OK not to have sex. The point is to become aware of some of your needs and unconscious drives and realize how you use sex to fulfill them. The clearer you are about all this the more you can get pleasure from sex when you have it, and be OK when you don't. And you can give up the expectation that sex will bring you what it can never provide. Sex is good and sex is natural. Just enjoy sex for what it is.

I'll bet that your attitudes about sex have changed a great deal since you were a boy. At least I hope so. Remember how intrigued (or obsessed) you were when you discovered sex? You thought about it all the time and you wanted it as much as you could. Maybe you still do! Some men get married because they think they will have sex any time they want. You already know how that turns out…. Sex can be a landmine in a marriage, an explosive source of frustration and conflict, if you don't update your attitudes and beliefs about it. So, let's keep exploring this mysterious, exciting subject.

FOCUS ON HER SATISFACTION
MORE THAN YOUR OWN

If you haven't updated your mental files, you may look at sex as an adolescent boy would: the more you have it the better; forget about your partner, just get off. If you approached sex this way, you have probably found that it doesn't work so well in marriage. For one thing, your wife may feel used. For another, you eventually find that it's not so fulfilling for you, either. In the young man's mind, women are objects for our enjoyment—and that's pretty much it. The problem is that youthful fantasies can wreck adult sex in marriage.

It's important that you look closely at your viewpoint of sex. You may have looked at sex as forbidden, dirty, violent or exploitative, or something very different. Whatever your attitude about it, that's what will drive sexuality in your marriage. In the '60s people used to talk about letting go of sexual "hang-ups." Few people did. In my experience, sexuality is often an unexplored territory. I want you to dig deeply into this fertile ground and let go of unhealthy patterns and ideas about sex. The key is to give up your expectations about it. Even the expectation that sex should be an expression of your mutual love will often disappoint you. Sex can be many things at many different times; it can't be put into a box and controlled.

One of the good things about marriage is that it gives you a relatively safe place to test and explore your sexuality. Marriage becomes an avenue for expansion of our whole mindset about sex and its place in our lives. We learn that sex may not provide the payoff we thought it would. We also learn that there's more to sex than just 'getting off.'

You can have better sex and fulfill your wife's needs and desires if you tune in to what she likes and needs instead of focusing on performance or orgasm as the main goal. Men like to have a goal, to feel useful and to solve a problem. During sex, make your wife's satisfaction and good feelings the goal, as well as your personal physical satisfaction. Even though you have a "goal," sex is the time to loosen up and enjoy the process along the way. You can do this best by making it an interaction of subtle give-and-take. During and after sex, notice your wife's likes and dislikes and don't be afraid to talk about them and learn. Every sexual experience is different. When you overlay your ideas of the way sex "has" to be you will only diminish your experience of it.

One key to good sex in marriage is to tune in to your wife's satisfaction. You may find that you have greater sexual fulfillment being a good lover for her than you ever had when you just wanted to have some release or to perform. This allows you to create ego-less love during sexual relations, which is more physically and emotionally satisfying for you both. Ego-less love means that you don't try to get anything out of the sexual experience, and you don't expect more out of it than it can give. You just enjoy the ride, care for your wife and then let it go. Remember, tune in to her, and it will work for you both.

SEXUAL POWER IS UNIVERSAL POWER

At the core of sexual energy is life energy, the primary power of the universe. Be aware of your male energy and explore it; sexual power is one expression of masculine power. Never be ashamed of your sexual, masculine energy, for at its core this is the universal energy that works through everything. This doesn't mean that sexuality is all-powerful. It means that sexual energy usually comes easily to us men. You should regard it as the same energy that gives you power and aliveness. Respect it as your life energy.

If sexual energy doesn't come easily to you, find out whether a physical problem is the reason. Many men are finding out that a low testosterone level is the culprit. On the other hand, different men simply have different levels of sexual interest and need, or different levels of sexual potency based on their physical and mental condition. There is no "right" level of sexual interest. If you are withholding sex to punish your wife, that's not right. If you want sex to make you feel better all the time, that's not right either. What is right is what is natural for you and what meets your needs and your wife's. Like all things in life and marriage, sexual frequency, duration and experience change over time. Let it change and let go of expectations.

Sex that expresses your essential, powerful, male energy is markedly different and much more fulfilling than sex out of neediness. This kind of sex is exciting, and when you ravish a woman this way she will be enthralled. Experiment with this: see if you can have sex while being aware of your sexual energy as raw male power.

There is no point in being attached to sex, however pleasurable sex may feel. As an old song once said, "When you're hot, you're hot; when you're not, you're not!" If you let your needs and demands for sex define your experience of life and marriage, you'll limit yourself more than you need to. You have to simultaneously embrace sex when you have it and let it go when you don't. Just enjoy sex when you can and how you can. You are not defined by your sexuality or your sexual desire. The only limit on you is your ability to tap into the universal power that flows through us all. Through your daily life and your marriage, you have the opportunity to access that power, which is your birthright.

BE THANKFUL SHE IS THERE WITH YOU FOR ANOTHER DAY

It's so easy to take your wife for granted. The things that used to seem so wonderful about her become old and unimportant. You stop seeing that she takes care to dress nicely, or takes your clothes to the cleaners, or cleans the house or a hundred other things that make your life better. And, if you're like most men, you no longer give her much recognition for what she does. The longer this goes on, the higher the bar is raised. What was once seen as terrific no longer gets noticed, and what was once OK becomes intolerable. This process leads only to frustration, anger, conflict and a difficult marriage.

It's easy to forget a fundamental fact of life—probably the fundamental fact of life: You may not be here tomorrow and she may not be here, either. There are no guarantees in life. Don't assume your marriage will last for many years or that you will have your wife's company forever. What if this was the last day of your life? What if you knew that your wife would be leaving you tomorrow, by death or some other reason? How would you treat her? What would you feel grateful for?

Decide to appreciate again the qualities you saw in your wife early in the marriage. Voice your appreciation for her and treat her with gratitude for the things she does around the house and the role she plays in your life. Be as courteous and nice to her as you would to an important client or customer. This is not a "technique." This is an internal attitude that keeps love alive and will bring you closer together. Tune in to your wife and begin to appreciate her again.

YOU'RE ON YOUR WAY

Many men don't pay attention to their marriages until it's too late to save them. Their marriages may be in a ditch with the grille bashed in, a tow truck pulling up, yellow lights flashing…and there they sit, blood on their foreheads, with a small smile, saying "Everything's fine, fine, my marriage is doing great, hand me the remote!"

Just by reading this book you're way ahead of the game. If you've gotten anything from this book, you've seen that it's time for action. It's no excuse to say, "But I'm a man, we don't know anything about marriage!" You can sit in the Barcalounger all day, numbed by ESPN and beer, but at some point you have to interact with your wife—or lose her.

It's time to move our marriages into the 21st century. The old ways of marriage stopped working about forty years ago and most of us haven't changed our thinking and behavior beyond "man provides and achieves; woman takes care of man and family." You now have the model you need to create a marriage for the 21st century, one based on love, trust and a spirit of mutual and individual freedom.

Stand strong with your vision of an "H" marriage: separate but equal, connected by the heart; a marriage based on commitment, honesty, fidelity and growth; one where neither partner expects the spouse to complete them or satisfy all their desires. Marriage can become your vehicle for mutual growth, and a fire to burn off your foolish ego. The emotional maturity you can gain through marriage allows you to become more whole. You will increase your capacity to experience love, and you'll become a better marriage partner.

I have urged you to create a "middle way" to be masculine in a marriage. Traditionally men did the thinking and women did the feeling in marriages. Recently, many women have become more aggressive while many men have become more passive and "feminine." This book has prescribed a path toward full masculinity, one that utilizes masculine energy to become a fully feeling and functioning person.

You know now that you have to be responsible for your own feelings and emotional patterns. Blaming and criticizing your wife for everything is the easiest thing in the world to do. It takes considerable courage to uncover and explore the source of your shame, anger, fear or other emotions. Regardless of who your partner is, the same emotional patterns will arise in you. My advice to you is: stay with your wife and learn about yourself.

We've also looked at some ways to "tune in to your wife," to meet some of her needs to be fully seen and appreciated. You've learned that part of your "marriage assignment" is to help further her growth as well as your own. You don't own your wife. Your job is to help her become freer, stronger and more fully herself. Your job isn't to "fix" her or always be there to take care of her. I hope you have seen the need for intimacy in your marriage; if so, you will do your part to communicate openly, honestly and clearly about your thoughts, needs and feelings.

Intimacy can hardly be overemphasized; creating an intimate connection is the key to have fulfilling sex with a woman. (Men have sex to connect; women want to connect before they have sex.) For men, sex is so often a way to express our inner emotions. Notice the emotion first—frustration, loneliness, sadness. Explore it; maybe even talk about it. At that point you may still have sex, but it will be a very different experience. Finally, I've described how important it is to focus on your wife's experience of sex, to give her pleasure throughout while also enjoying sex as an expression of your masculine power.

So many men are asleep to their own feelings and hearts! They walk through life numbed and out of touch with themselves. Take this opportunity to commit yourself to a life of energy, exploration and inner courage. Please don't waste this book—and don't waste your marriage. Utilize your marriage as the primary crucible for your growth. It won't be easy; you'll have conflicts and rough periods along the way. At times you may want to leave the marriage. You may even wish you'd never met your wife. Persevere through those times, keep the focus on you and your application of my three steps, and you'll succeed.

May your marriage be a rich source of joy for you and your wife, and may you continue to grow toward inner freedom.

CHAPTER FIVE

For Women: Secrets of the Married Man's Mind

MEN IN MARRIAGE

You might think I'm a little crazy. I am devoting my life to something a lot of people say is impossible. I want to change the way men look at their relationships, and the entire way they act in their marriages. As you can imagine, a great many men don't want what I have to give, and it's pretty frustrating sometimes not to be able to help while watching a marriage fall apart. Most men don't want to think about relationships and they certainly don't want to talk about them, either; they're scared, wary and blissfully ignorant. As a consequence, they avoid learning about the very thing that would bring more meaning to their lives. I know that what I have to say works, because the ideas and tools in this book have changed my life and the lives of other men, too. But, I need your help to get the man in your life to take a look at what's inside this book.

I make a great many points about how men and women act and think. You probably know people who are exceptions to the generalizations I make. Perhaps you are the exception. Men and women have unique characteristics, common to their sex, that are deeply rooted in their psyches. But not all people act them out. As in most things, there is a bell-shaped curve at work; some will fall on either side of the curve, but the overwhelming majority of people will fall in the middle. It's not my intention to be dogmatic about these differences between men and women; I do understand that there are many, many exceptions even if I don't mention them. I ask for your understanding and forgiveness of my generalizations about men and women.

As a woman, you are the relationship expert; not your man. You have more natural interest and ability in the realm of relationships than most men do. You can see and talk about subtle dimensions of feelings and interactions that most men don't even understand. It may be a cliché that women are better at relationships than men, but in my experience it's true. The question I want to discuss with you is: why do so many relationships and marriages fail? Is it because men are so clueless and uninterested? To a very large degree, the answer is yes! But it's more complicated than that, and it's not all your man's fault. Really!

If men were as good as women at communication and intimacy, more marriages would succeed. No doubt about it. Of course, men aren't and marriages don't, and at least half of the marriages in the U.S. fail. Many marriages do survive, but not very well. I know it's frustrating to deal with your man sometimes. If he's like most married men, he wants his marriage to be easy and he probably doesn't want to put much effort or time into making it work. Many men, without thinking about it too much, expect their wives to take care of the home, the kids, and to a great extent, their own emotional life— without their help. It can feel like you have to be a combination of social planner, maid, mommy, counselor and a lot more, while your husband just expects the relationship to take care of itself.

You know, of course, that relationships don't just take care of themselves; they take a great deal of work, and they are constantly evolving. Men think relationships should be like buying a refrigerator: you buy one, set it up and can use it for years and years without having to worry about maintaining or cleaning it. Every time you try to talk to a man about "the relationship" he is surprised because he thought it was all "set." He thinks you are just finding fault, looking for problems, and instantly he feels defensive because he knows you are going to tell him he's wrong somehow.

We haven't even touched on the issue of sex. Men expect sex, yet most of them aren't willing to establish a sufficiently intimate connection with you to get it. That can be a real turn-off and a source of major conflicts. Too many men neglect to create an emotional connection with their women. It's understandable if you feel used or neglected sometimes. Later on, I'm going to tell you about how men look at sex and what they use it for, and you may be surprised by what I have to say.

At my speeches and workshops, I often meet women who are working overtime to create a good marriage. They are desperately miserable because their husbands are driven workaholics, lost in the pursuit of a career. Or because these men refuse to participate in simple household chores, or meaningful conversations, while losing themselves instead in sports, hobbies, projects, the internet or television. Or because they are so divorced from their feelings that they've become like zombies, cut off from their own pain and emotions. Amazingly, these same men won't talk about their marriages or seek help. They'd rather deny that their marriage is in trouble, although obviously they need to change.

You may have noticed, however, that no matter how many times you criticize, complain or even ask your husband nicely, your man doesn't change in any fundamental way. There are four possible reasons why men don't change: a) They don't see a reason to change (Why would you change your refrigerator if it's still working?); b) they don't know how to change; c) they fear that if they tried to change they would fail, and they would feel ashamed for not performing; or, d) they don't change because you are the one pushing them to change. As much as a man might love his woman, he's got too much invested in his male ego to change just because you tell him to.

So I know how frustrating and difficult it can be to try to get a man to shift his attitudes and actions about relationships. But the thing is, I believe in men. We men have so many great natural gifts to draw upon to create a great marriage or relationship. There is nothing like masculine power unleashed to solve problems and move mountains; the last thing you'd want is for your man to lose his powerful male energy. In this book, I show men how they can be full participants in their marriage without becoming less of a man. Your husband urgently needs to have a step-by-step relationship road map that has been designed by another married man—not a therapist. He needs a complete guide that he can follow and that will make him feel and be successful. I'll make you a promise: If your man reads and applies the principles in this book, he'll change his life and his marriage, and thus yours, too, in a radical way. Can you imagine what that would be like?

You'd have a husband who was fully in your marriage. He'd pay more attention and listen to you better. He'd appreciate more of what you do for the household and the marriage. He'd learn to be more vulnerable and intimate with you, and that would dramatically improve your communication and sex life. You'd have a man who took responsibility for his own feelings and needs; he'd be more interested in exploring his inner life and less interested in blaming you for his troubles. He'd pull his own weight in the marriage and get up off the couch to pitch in. And, just as important, your man would be masculine. You'd feel his masculine energy and be more attracted to it.

This may sound unlikely to you, but I know it can be done. I've done it myself. I'm still learning how to be a man in a marriage, but I can tell you it's far more fulfilling this way than when I was zoned out and uninvolved, sleepwalking through life. I worked for twenty-five years as a management consultant, teaching managers how to deal with communication and relationship issues in the corporate world. I was sailing along, completely unaware of the condition of my marriage, when I was blindsided by my wife. She announced that she wanted out of the marriage, and it sent me into a tailspin. In the middle of that disorientation I realized, with incredible clarity, that I hadn't been fully present in the marriage and had gotten way out of touch with myself. I've since had many, many insights about how I could participate in the marriage differently, and I've found the potential for a different kind of a marriage. I began to share my viewpoint with other men, and I discovered that I could apply my former expertise about communication and relationships to the marriage context. I'm glad to say that I'm still married, and married in a much more powerful way. I'm also very excited that I'm helping many married men become more engaged and skillful partners with their wives.

CHANGES IN MARRIAGE

Women have moved through many changes over the past forty years, becoming more powerful and independent. Like most women, you are probably less willing to settle for a lousy marriage than were women of your mother's generation. Too many men haven't kept up. They are still holding on to the old model for marriage: the man provides for the woman; the woman takes care of the man, the home and the children. That model served humanity well for thousands of years, and some marriages can still make it work. Most women struggle with it. You have a tremendous burden not only to meet or accommodate many of the old model's expectations but also to make your way in the world, be equal to men and become self-fulfilled. That's a lot to live up to!

Many women and some men, as well, view the old model as too limiting. We need a new model to guide us in the 21st century when so much about life and relationships is in flux. Up until the 1970s divorce was relatively rare. As you know, divorce is so common now that it hardly raises an eyebrow. We need a set of expectations for marriage that will radically alter the way we view marriage and that will keep us interested and committed to the marriage for a lifetime. That's what this book is about.

A great marriage is one that is alive with growth. It may be difficult and challenging and have conflict and strife, but the participants stay in the marriage because they have the understanding that learning to confront their egos and to open up to more love is the purpose of marriage. They know that marriage is all about learning to love another person, even though your ego may tell you otherwise. That kind of marriage eventually becomes a vehicle for each person's psychological, emotional and spiritual development. Romance might come and go, your children will grow up and leave, but you make communication, honesty, support and love the constants. And you are committed to your marriage out of integrity, not merely to please society, parents or anyone else. In this kind of marriage, we eventually abandon the notion that our partner is the key to our happiness. Instead, we utilize the sacred container of marriage to help us become a stronger, more loving person.

VALUING MEN

With your permission, I would like to share with you some tips for how to deal with men in a marriage or long-term relationship. As I mentioned, men are great; you just need to know how to work with us instead of against us. The first thing I want to suggest to you is that you swear off all male-bashing. That means the next time one of your women friends starts a conversation with, "My husband is such an idiot..." you refuse to jump in with your own stories that demonstrate that your own man is also a "factory second." I want you to see beyond the stereotype of the dumb man.

Men are great warriors, problem-solvers, competitors and innovators. We have evolved to be hunters and to protect our women and children. Give a man a task he can succeed at and he will find a way to achieve it. In other words, we love to perform, to look outward and make our way in the world. Our natural inclination is to produce results rather than to look inside at the world of feelings and intuition. It would be great if you could fully value how your husband takes care of you and your family, and by that I don't necessarily mean as the income earner. Obviously, in today's society, many women are working, too. But most men take care of their wives in many other ways, by doing the "dirty work" at home, such as killing spiders and mice, making repairs, taking care of the car's maintenance and doing yard work. More importantly, I have never met a man yet who didn't feel pressure to make money for his family and to protect them physically. You may not realize it but that pressure is no small thing for men to carry around. Men desperately want to protect their women from pain. Our driving motivation is to help, protect and serve our women and to provide safety and to nurture them in the ways we know how.

Here is the way many men feel: We take care of women in tangible, worthwhile ways, and instead of thanks we often get ridicule and disrespect from women and the media. In greeting cards, situation comedies, commercials, advertisements and male- bashing jokes, men are portrayed as useless idiots and jerks. Please begin to accept and appreciate what men can do, and refuse to discard your man as being useless or broken. None of us can create good marriages if we lack mutual respect and compassion.

One key to understanding men is this: We want to be heroes. You may think this is silly, but from a man's viewpoint it's real and important. If you can figure out how to let your man feel like a hero, you will always have a happier man. Thankfully, this doesn't mean that a man can't learn to be more at home with the unseen, inner world— it just means that it usually doesn't come as naturally to us. We are fallible human beings, just like you. So my message is: Let your man be a man; please don't make him wrong for not being like a woman.

In my seminars and speeches I often ask men for their biggest complaints about women. In nearly every case, these boil down to the same two things. Can you guess what they are? The top two things: too much criticism and not enough sex.

CRITICISM AND CHANGE

You will be glad to know that I always tell men that they can greatly lessen the criticism they get if they will begin to listen better and take action to change. However, I'm often struck by how little women understand the power of their criticism, how it drives men away, hurts and shames them. Your man will not tell you that he feels ashamed. But, believe me, he does. You should see the heads nod when I talk to groups of men about shame and criticism. Here's what you should know: nearly any time a man gets the idea that he hasn't pleased you or hasn't performed, he will feel shame. Too much shame and your man will withdraw or lash out. You will lose, and so will he, and so will your children. Everything, from your work life to your love life to your sex life, will suffer.

Many women are more committed to making their man wrong than making him right. Criticism sometimes becomes the norm, not the exception, and the criticism sounds bitter and nasty. If you want your man to change, but make him wrong through your criticism, it will create far more problems than it will solve. At the same time, a man genuinely needs a woman's coaching and help to get better. Whether he knows it or not, that's one of the primary reasons he married you!

What men don't realize is that your criticism comes from a genuinely worthwhile intention. You see the potential in your man, and you naturally want him to improve. You see how his ego holds him back and how much greater he could be. Strangely enough, men don't see the potential in their women; in fact, when you got married, your man was probably hoping you wouldn't change, if he thought about it at all. But, like all women, you draw on a naturally ferocious power that smashes pretense and the falseness of the ego in your man. The trouble comes when you get so angry or frustrated that your criticism turns vicious and begins to cut deeper and deeper. When you go "over the top" with your criticism, it will cause a man to turn off entirely or to lash out with equal vehemence. Either way, you won't get what you want. What is the alternative?

Instead of giving your husband the kind of biting criticism that destroys far more than it improves, remember that men: 1) love to be accepted and appreciated, and 2) are built to perform tasks. So, here's what I recommend: If you want your man to do something different, make a simple, specific request and give him appreciation if he accomplishes the task. Before you criticize, think, "What do I specifically want?" Come up with concrete things for your man to do, and ask him to do them. Men love to please women, and they will continue to try to please as long as they know what to do—unless, of course, they are told what to do. Criticism and complaints communicate that you're not pleased but they don't tell a man what to do, and that's what he needs to hear if you want him to change. For example, instead of saying, "I'm not your maid! You never do anything around here!" you might say, "Would you please load your dishes in the dishwasher after you have a snack at night? I'm pretty tired at night and it would help me a lot if you'd do that."

Men feel safe enough to listen and to change when they sense that they are loved unconditionally. Your man will change faster with loving acceptance and sweet words than with criticism. You have a right to ask for what you want, and if you ask without rancor and with love, you will very likely get it, especially if you show him how much you appreciate what he did. This is, of course, easier to say than to do.

Please be watchful for your own issues of control, criticism and resentment; they will only pollute your well-intended constructive feedback. Many women criticize men because of their own uncompleted issues about their father and other men. It's easy to project onto your man your feelings of anger, hurt, lack of appreciation or any abusive treatment that came from other men. I hope you will do your best to criticize your man in a caring manner. When you criticize or give feedback out of your own lack of self-esteem or hurt feelings from the past, you will most likely receive angry feelings back. Do your best to work out those issues outside of your relationship, or enroll your husband into allowing you to work them out with him. In other words, please make sure your criticism is only to help your husband and not about reacting to your father or other men from your past. You may not think you do this but every woman does it at one time or another, either consciously or unconsciously; so please take a hard look to see if it applies to you.

TAKING CARE OF A MAN

I mentioned earlier that men often expect their women to manage their emotional care and feeding. Many women gladly take responsibility for their husband's diet, physical health and clothes. They also make a project out of their husband's inner life and emotional growth. This is a double-edged sword.

It feels good to take care of your man this way. You feel needed, and he'll rely on you for emotional support, and to the extent that he is able to talk about his feelings, he'll talk about them with you. In fact, you are probably the only person to whom he can talk that openly. And, of course, helping your man this way is playing to your strength. Many women, on the other hand, greatly resent being in charge of their husband's inner life. And, in the long run, it is not the best thing for your man or your marriage because it weakens both of you. I want you to feel like a wife, not a mommy, around your husband. Therefore, I recommend that you gradually stop taking care of your man's feelings, his emotional well-being and personal growth.

Changing your approach this way may take some time and some real work on your part, but I know you will benefit, as will your husband. In the long run, no woman is strengthened by being mommy or therapist to her husband, and no man is either. Men do need help sometimes and they know that women have greater access to the world of emotions. Helping your man by listening and encouraging him is one thing; taking responsibility for his inner life is another. When you do, it robs him of the chance to stand on his own two feet and steals from you the chance to be a separate, strong person of your own. Any man would appreciate it if you give him tenderness, caring and empathy, and he'll value your observations and comments. You don't need to stop giving nurturance; in fact, I hope you don't. Just be clear that his emotions are his. It is not your job to change your mate; it's your role to support his own growth. Be a help-mate, not a mommy.

COMMUNICATING WITH A MAN

I wrote a good deal in this book that helps men learn how to listen, talk, be less defensive and resolve conflict better. Men have their own unique way of communication. Please don't expect a man to communicate like a woman. He will usually say less about what he feels than any woman would; he may not say anything at all. This doesn't mean that he doesn't feel anything. It just means that he either doesn't feel comfortable talking about the issue or feeling, or that he doesn't know what he feels. The more you demand that he talk about his feelings your way, the worse he will feel. He'll feel shame because he can't perform, and anger that you are pushing him.

While we're on the subject, I want to mention how men feel about "relationship" talks. We hate them. Men generally don't put a high priority on managing their relationships or marriages, and most men don't want to talk about them. Relationships are important to men, but we want our love relationships to be easy places of refuge and we don't want to put a great deal of energy into figuring the relationship out or improving it, unless we know what to do. We figure our woman will tell us if the relationship isn't working, and she'll also tell us how to fix it if it's broken.

HOW TO TALK TO YOUR MAN ABOUT YOUR RELATIONSHIP

When you start a conversation about "the relationship" it seems natural and necessary to you. It gets the issues out on the table, and you believe that the process of talking will reveal important issues and feelings. To a man, any conversation about the relationship seems scary and unfamiliar, likely to be a waste of time at best and a painful disaster at the worst. He's not going in with an attitude of "Hey, what a great idea—let's talk about the relationship! I'll go first!" Nope—all he's thinking about is damage control. He wants to get the conversation over with as quickly as possible— with the least amount of emotional pain.

What does a man want in a relationship conversation? Aside from brevity, he wants the conversation to solve a specific problem. A general relationship conversation is confusing. He immediately feels somewhat out of control, on foreign territory. He's on the hot seat. A man's first thought is: "What did I do wrong?" Then, "What does she mean?" "What does she want out of me?" "Why is she talking so much, and where is this going?" And most important, "What can I do to get this over with?"

Please don't expect your man to analyze and discuss "the relationship" in general terms. If you ask a man how the relationship is going, he'll usually say, "Fine," and think that's enough! He most likely can't and won't do it your way, and it will only make him mad if you ask him to, because he's likely to feel that he can't perform in that situation. Instead, in a calm and loving way request specifically what you want from him and make the discussion about what you need and want. Remember, men want to know how to perform successfully. Rather than saying, "I need more attention and caring," you might say, "It would mean a lot to me if we could spend this Sunday morning together and go out for a bite to eat and just catch up about our week." Rather than saying, "You are always bringing work home and you never leave any time for your family," you might say, "I really miss your energy around here. Would you be willing to be available to the family after eight o'clock most nights?"

Keep the conversation short and to the point; from a man's perspective, the longer the conversation the worse it will be. Make sure your man knows that you value his good intentions; the fact that he cares and wants things to work is worth mentioning. Another critical suggestion is to avoid the use of the words "never" and "always," because they inflame the conversation and preclude the possibility of change. If you say, for example, "You never take the trash out!" your husband will likely become angry simply because he knows he has taken the trash out a few times. You can substitute words like "frequently," "very often" or "seldom" instead of using "never" and "always."

COMMUNICATION AND INTIMACY

As you know, we men often find it difficult to talk fluently about our feelings. We are built to focus intently on our task, so we keep our attention outward and in a straight line. We tend to approach things in a rational, sequential way. Women, of course, can entertain many things at once in their minds and they usually can tune in to the realms of intuition and feelings more easily than men can. Scientists tell us that men's brains are simply wired a little differently than women's.

There are also social influences at work here. We men learn to put on armor to hide our feelings. We are told from an early age to "be a man," and not to be a "sissy." Many of us were told to not act "like a girl," which we translated to, "Don't show your feelings or vulnerability." In fact, many men associate revealing their feelings with being feminine and so are deeply ashamed when their most vulnerable feelings are revealed. Some men adopt a stoic, stone-faced demeanor while others hide behind a tough, macho façade. Some men become super humorous and use the "funny-man" role to hide behind. However we men put ourselves forward, you can bet there is some suffering underneath the pretense.

Many men are suffering very badly in our society yet won't admit it, perhaps even to themselves. Most men want to provide for their families—that's in our genetic makeup. We want to be strong and to protect our families, too. On the other hand, men are constantly portrayed in the media as dolts and idiots. In much of modern civilized society we are told to show our soft side and not to be like men of previous generations. The only problem is that when we do this we are often shot down as weak and wimpy, even by the women we love.

Have you ever seen a good movie about a sensitive, aware man in touch with his feelings while still being strongly masculine? Neither have I. Instead, we get super-heroes and tough cops and gangsters. Or, we see weak, burned-out, "sensitive" men who have lost their ability to be warriors in the best sense of the word. Our society hasn't created a positive and acceptable way for men to be men, and we need a way to be a new kind of husband as well. It's no wonder that many men pour all of their energy into their work; at least there they know how to be successful and powerful and be validated for it. So please have compassion for your man's struggles. They're not yours, but they are still important. I ask you to never look down on a man for not being like a woman.

If you want your man to drop his armor and be more intimate, he will have to trust you. He will have to be convinced that he won't be shamed or criticized or belittled, regardless of what he says or how well or poorly he says it. He will have to work up to letting his guard down by testing your acceptance in many small ways. One thing is sure: if you make your man wrong for not talking about his feelings your way, he will simply shut down. For a man, an intimate conversation with a woman can feel like he is supposed to perform on command. "Now, talk about your feelings—and do it exactly this way!" That's belittling and counterproductive. It feels like we are supposed to do a parlor trick for you, on your terms. You can call it the fragile male ego if you want, and you may think it's silly, but to us it's not. Men need to maintain their dignity.

Allow your man to talk about his troubles his own way for a while. It can be excruciating when your man tells you a long, factual story about work, when all you want to know is: How do you feel about it? It's probably not that he is hiding his feelings from you. He simply doesn't know how he feels! If you watch him closely, he will gradually demonstrate what he feels. After he talks on the surface of things for a while, he will eventually tell you what matters to him. Let him simply feel accepted and heard for a while. If it feels right, you can summarize what you've heard him say and talk about what you sense he's feeling. But I wouldn't recommend hitting him with, "So how do you feel about that?" If you demand everything said in a "feminine" way, he will think that he's being told he's wrong, that he's not performing. You will soon have a man who feels like a failure at intimacy and relationships, one who may become even harder to reach.

If you want communication that is rich, deep and soulful, I recommend that you talk to other women. Your female friends can give you the kind of sensitive, intuitive contact you crave and deserve. In today's world, you have to work harder than in years past to create a community of women; everyone is so busy and geographically dispersed and isolated. I think women need to be together sometimes without men, and men need to be together with other men so that they can act like men. When women get together and communicate, they share deeply personal feelings on many levels. When male friends get together and communicate, the male energy bounces off the walls and it probably will look very messy and sound very loud and the topics will probably not be that personal. If personal issues are discussed, you can bet the conversation will be brief and simple, at least compared to the way women relate to each other. Yet it's just as important for men to hang out together as it is for women.

Again, I recommend that you give up any expectation that your man will talk and listen in the same way as women. You'll be happier if you appreciate the differences in communication.

APPRECIATION AND POWER

Let me tell you something else about men. Men show their love by performing tasks for you. In ancient times, men would bring their daily "kill" from hunting back to the tribe and show it off, especially to the women present. Believe me, we often feel the same way today; we want to show off what we've done for you. Most men want to work hard, for themselves and their families. Even if you are the major breadwinner, it would be to your advantage if occasionally you would tell your man how much you appreciate his contribution to your lives together. A man may love his work, but there is a large part of him that thinks he's making a sacrifice for his family—and he wants to be acknowledged for it. If a man goes out of his way to move the furniture for you, he is doing it for you, not just to improve the looks of the house. If he stops off at the store on the way home and picks up a flavor of ice cream that he knows you like, he is doing it for you, because he loves you. If you let these gestures go by without comment, you are missing a great opportunity.

Never underestimate the powerful impact your positive encouragement and appreciation has on a man. Your heartfelt appreciation for his actions will make him want to work harder to please you. Give your husband sincere, kind words or a sweet touch for how well he performs at sex, work, housework and communication. Tell him when he looks good, too, and he'll probably dress better (he may ask for your help). Appreciation will bring you much that's good. You can get almost anything you want from a man if you talk to him with kindness and compassion, let him feel good about himself and help him feel loved.

It's certainly OK to make your points and argue when you need to; your marriage absolutely needs conflict if it's going to thrive. Healthy conflict is what brings change to a marriage. So, by all means, speak your mind and stand up for yourself. It's not about giving in to him and letting him win at your expense. I ask you, however, to avoid the temptation to give "or else" threats or to hammer your man with accusations. Use your power to uplift yourself, not to tear your man down.

We will create better relationships in the 21st century if we base them on equality of power. Otherwise, women are merely playing into the old game that men are more powerful and in control at the expense of women's own power. Many women are fighting tooth and nail to get their own power back; it's rare that women find their own power at their fingertips. Here's what I tell men: "You need to help your woman to become fully powerful; it's ultimately to your own benefit!" Of course, numerous men are threatened by the shift in power in their relationships. That's why I want you to know: Give your man appreciation, kindness and compassion, and he will support change in your marriage, including the increase in your personal power.

RELATIONSHIPS AND FANTASIES

Is your marriage filled with exciting fireworks? It's so easy in our society to think that a relationship is the key to happiness. To the extent that women (or men) want constant romance and fireworks within marriage, they will be disappointed. According to many women's magazines you should have great sex, romantic, candlelit evenings, intimate conversations and caring trust with your husband—and have it frequently. You should also be able to easily balance your career, parental responsibilities and emotional needs. It seems to me that women's magazines make problems seem all too easy—just take a soothing, hot bubble bath and everything will be fine!

If you are like most women, you probably have some fairy-tale ideas about love and marriage that date from childhood. A handsome man on a beautiful white horse will sweep you off your feet and you will live "happily ever after." Every filmed romantic comedy reinforces some form of this old idea. Have you ever noticed that all those movies end with the deliriously happy couple before they get married and have to live with each other? Unfortunately, the reality of marriage seldom measures up to the fantasy.

Very few men are as devoted as their wives are to keeping romance and excitement alive in their marriage. As I mentioned earlier, most men just want their marriages to be easy places of refuge. We men often want to be off duty when we are home, and we generally don't think about romance unless our wives tell us to think about it. This is not to say that men don't want excitement, connection and love in their marriages. What I'm saying is that our minds naturally travel in other directions. Look, even if you are married to the world's most romantic man, the everyday drudgery of life will get in the way of marital bliss. When the sink is full of dirty dishes and the toilet is plugged up, it's hard to maintain a fairy-tale life.

Many women blame their men when their relationships don't fit their fantasies. It's usually the fault of the fantasy more than the fault of the man or the woman. I urge you to give up your pictures of a "perfect" relationship and accept the relationship you have. It's true that men are flawed and relationships with them are difficult; however, a woman can gain a great deal from being with a man. And, women are flawed and relationships with them are difficult, too.

Living with a man will inevitably reveal emotional issues about your father and other men in your life, if you are willing to face these issues. You also need a man to balance your feminine energy; masculine and feminine together create a whole. Perhaps most important, marriage can teach you how to love another human being fully and unconditionally, and in the process learn to love yourself. Selfish, dependent, clinging love will ruin a marriage; unconditional love exalts it. You can learn how to love like that through using the challenges that marriage gives you. I hope you will find your own needs and your own path in life and use marriage to help you understand yourself better. Your quest for your true, feminine self may take you in spiritual, psychological and emotional directions. Just remember that your ultimate happiness won't come from your man.

If your man is abusive or violent, you should leave him. If your man doesn't share your most critical values, again, leave the marriage. Otherwise, I believe that you are better off staying with the man you've got, and using the marriage to teach you many of the life-lessons you need to learn. If you divorce your husband and re-marry, you will be horrified to see most of your old emotional issues arise once more. You will surely carry your emotional weaknesses with you wherever you go, as will your husband.

I knew a woman who was married to a very private, intense man. She wanted emotional connection and frequent and deep conversations, while he wanted time alone. She begged him to talk, and berated him frequently because he didn't share enough of his feelings with her. She had a great opportunity to learn about her need to try to control people and situations to fit her expectations. She could have discovered many things from that relationship if she could have kept it together, and he could have learned how to reveal more of his inner life and to rely on others. Sadly, after only a few years together, they split up when things got tough.

We all want to change the person we are married to, rather than turning our attention to ourselves. That's why I say that improving the relationship starts with improving yourself. You will find fault with your husband to the extent that you are unhappy with yourself. It's not that he doesn't have faults; we all do. If you pay attention, marriage will give you the situations that allow you to discover your own contribution to your pain. As you learn more about your own emotional patterns from the past, you gradually learn to stop blaming and criticizing your husband because, eventually, it becomes clear that he is not the main cause of your problem. Of course, exactly the same thing goes for your husband, and I go into great detail about that in this book.

One woman married her husband because he was a steady, grounded man who could provide a good home and financial security. Now she complains that he isn't enough fun and should talk about his feelings more. I know another woman who married a fun-loving man who was constantly on the move. Now she criticizes him for not staying at home more, and for being too childish. These examples tell you something important: The very things that drive you crazy now are probably what attracted you to your man in the first place. It would be great if you could learn to appreciate the man you have, and to forgive him for his faults. This approach works well if you give up the idea that your marriage is the key to your happiness; perhaps the greatest illusion in life is the idea that a person, place or thing can give us lasting happiness.

MANAGING THE RELATIONSHIP

Now, let me be blunt. If you want a long-term marriage please recognize that you are more tuned-in to the overall well-being of the relationship than your partner is, and therefore you are ideally suited to manage the relationship. My guess is that you already monitor the health of your marriage and are aware of subtle nuances that your husband is unconscious of. A typical man won't spend more than a minute or two a day reflecting upon his marriage, unless things are going extremely well or extremely badly. Even at your most stressed, you are aware of far more about your relationship than your husband is. He may know about some of the problems. But his response is mainly to acknowledge that some things are messed up, and then to move on to other matters. It's a rare man who's got a handle on all the variables in his relationship and feels responsible for it. He knows you have more interest and skill at the relationship, so he stakes a claim on different turf and leaves the relationship arena to you.

If you read my book for men, you will see that one of my main points is that men need to create a vision for the kind of marriage they want and commit to it with all of their hearts. I want men to stand steady in the storms of marriage. Another large part of the book stresses that men need to take responsibility for their side of the marriage. So please understand that I want your man to be just as accountable for the marriage as you are. I want men to stand up for their marriages in a much more powerful, committed way. I want them to be "warriors" in their marriages, and I define that term very carefully, so that men have a role they are suited to. I want men to be fiercely committed to a lofty, righteous vision of marriage. But I don't want them to try to manage the relationship.

As I indicated, your relationship will work best when you take over its management; men are notoriously poor at managing relationships. I know that this might seem like a huge weight to shoulder, in addition to all the things you already carry. I'm not trying to drag you down. Actually, I want to free you up, and empower you to do what you are best at. I want you to manage the relationship without feeling guilty or resentful that your husband isn't equally bought into it.

Don't misunderstand his lack of interest in talking about the relationship; it doesn't mean he doesn't care. If he's like ninety-nine percent of the men I know, he wants to have a good marriage and he does care. He simply doesn't know what to do about his marriage. That's why I recommend that you become much clearer about what needs to be done, and take the reins to make sure it happens.

Managing the relationship doesn't mean that you are superior to your man; there's no room here for condescension or fault-finding. I hope you don't become a dictator, issuing a never-ending stream of orders. Believe me, that will backfire on you quickly, because it steals from your man his dignity and builds resentment. I am talking about only one thing: doing what it takes to make sure your relationship works.

Let's look at one important part of a marriage: housework. We all know that men "should" do housework that is equal to their wife's. That's only fair. How many men actually do their half of the work? Nearly every woman I know does more housework than her man, and even if he "pitches in" she's still in charge of the overall home. However, as Warren Farrell says in *Women Can't Hear What Men Don't Say* (an excellent book), men work hard around the house on their days off, doing repairs, chores and projects, and they may do "administrative" work, such as paying bills and handling other financial matters. It's not that men don't do work around the house; for some, anyway, it's more that the work they do isn't classified as "housework."

Nevertheless, if a woman is typical, she often resents the fact that she does so much of the work while her husband is off duty, watching TV, fooling around on the internet or out of the house entirely. A man may not care as much as you about housework, but he will care a lot about pleasing you if he knows what to do to make you happy (or stop you from criticizing him). Your first step is to compile a list of chores and either assign him some or let him choose what he will do on a regular basis.

Ask for help with the chores in a loving way and tell him how much it will mean to you; then make him feel appreciated for what he does. A man would much rather do household tasks for the well-being of his relationship or to please his wife than he ever would do such chores simply for the well-being of his home. Again, men "should" take on equal household tasks. If your man doesn't, there's no sense calling him a male chauvinist pig. Instead of blaming or criticizing him, manage the relationship and the tasks to be done around the house and make sure that you tell him how much you appreciate him for the work he does on evenings and weekends that you probably wouldn't or couldn't do and may take for granted.

Here's another example of managing the relationship. Most women wish their husbands would listen to them better and show them more appreciation for all they do. You could blame your man for not doing these things, or you could look more closely at what you've done to contribute to the situation and what you might do to improve it. As you know, when men listen they often don't fully hear you. Before you've even completed your main point they may well interrupt and try to solve your "problem," failing to empathize at the level you want and need. So here's what I recommend: If you have something important to say, tell your husband what you need from him, and tell him when you don't need anything but his presence.

As strange as it may seem, we need to know: Do you want us to give you advice? Be a shoulder to cry on? Help you understand your own mixed-up thoughts and feelings? Or just sit there and keep quiet and be a sounding board. Again, men "should" listen better, and this book gives them the listening tools they need. However, rather than waiting for your man to learn to become a good listener, manage the situation and tell him what you need from him as a listener.

Maybe one more example would make the concept of managing a relationship more clear. I knew a woman who was in absolute despair about her husband because he was always gone, working hard to build a business. They had small children at home and she really needed his support, but from his point of view he was doing the right thing—attempting to provide for his family. The more she confronted him about always being gone, the angrier they both became—and he continued to stay away. He made time for a weekly night out with his male friends, but refused to budget more time for his wife and kids. Now, if I were talking to that man I'd have to restrain myself not to slap him in the head! I'd want to tell him, "Snap out of it! You're in danger of losing your whole family! Go home to your wife and take your marriage seriously!" But I'm addressing the woman's side of the equation here.

Men are fairly simple. Your man will want to be with you in the way you desire only if you make him feel appreciated and loved and accepted. If he feels like a hero at home he'll want to stay with you and give you what you want. In the example above, that man was greeted at home with a constant barrage of criticism and conflict about his work schedule. Even when she scheduled "fun" time for them together, she made sure that they talked about their relationship and her many complaints. In a way, I can understand why he stayed away—his experience of home was chaos and criticism.

If she were managing the relationship, she could have given him much appreciation for his hard work while telling him how much he mattered to her and what she needed to feel more connected to him. She could have made sure they had some fun together, without the kids, when relationship talk was off-limits. She could have asked for a specific amount of time with him every week, and obtained an agreement from him for his evening arrival times. Finally, she could have given him sexual experiences that would make him want to be intimate with her, even if they were both tired. (More on sex, in a moment.)

I know you may not be sure of exactly what you want and need in many aspects of your life or marriage. That's not surprising, and many women are struggling to understand their needs in a way that men don't. My point is simple: the more you know about what you really want, the more you can ask for it and receive it in your marriage.

Let's turn now to an extremely important issue for most men: sex. I want to tell you how men understand and experience sex, and how you might want to respond.

MEN, MARRIAGE AND SEX

I mentioned earlier that men consistently have two major concerns about their marriages: too much criticism and not enough sex. Of course, men are often surprised to find that some women are concerned about the frequency and quality of the sex in their marriages, too. You probably know that sex is vitally important to most men. We are biologically programmed to seek multiple sexual partners and to have sex frequently. Our first instinct upon seeing a woman is to assess her as a sexual partner; we are easily aroused through visual stimuli, whether live or in still or moving pictures. You may find this repulsive or wrong, but it's simply what men do.

It may seem that men are simply animals, driven by biological urges, and that may sometimes be true, especially for younger men. What you may not fully understand is that men may want sex for other reasons, reasons that the men themselves are very likely unaware of.

Here's an important point: Men have sex to connect to their women—and to themselves. First and foremost, men use sex to connect to you; it's their way to be intimate. Deep conversation doesn't do it. Stroking and touching don't do it. Long walks by the river don't do it. Dining by candlelight doesn't do it. For most men, only sex really means intimacy with you. It's very hard for a man to feel fully connected to you without sex. He may jump through a lot of hoops that you create for him to show that he really cares about you—and he does really care about you. But for a man, the shortest and best route to intimacy with you is when you're having sex with him; in fact, for some men it may be the only experience of intimacy they have access to.

Your man may want to have sex with you to express emotions that he can't or won't talk about, or even acknowledge to himself. Men may use sex as a way to act out or react to sadness, loss, grief, failure, frustration, love, joy or many, many other things he feels. These unconscious responses stem from childhood patterns a man may develop with his parents, siblings or other loved ones. For example, old, uncontrollable feelings of insecurity from childhood may be triggered by a man's rejection at work. He might then use sex to soothe the feeling and express it, unaware of what is behind his strong desire for sex. Sometimes sex is just sex. Other times it's to work things out or to connect with you. Either way, it's important to a man.

So here's the dilemma: You usually want intimacy before you'll have sex, and he usually wants intimacy through having sex. What can you do? Let me start with what not to do. You can ruin sex for a man in many ways. For instance, criticize his performance. Talk about household chores or worries when it's time to be sexually intimate. Act as if you are doing him a favor by having sex with him. Or withhold sex often, and grant him sex only for "special" occasions. And most important not to do: keep all the power and make him a beggar for sex.

Here's what I recommend you do: Move in his direction and then get him to move toward yours. Allow your man to have sex as an expression of his male power, and sometimes just because he needs it. I am not suggesting that you should have sex wherever and whenever your husband wants it. I want you to feel free to choose the place and time you'll have sex, but I recommend that you do it often enough to keep your man interested and happy. During sex you can demonstrate what feels good to you, without making him wrong, and over time you can create more intimacy before sex as well.

It's a good idea to take performance out of the equation; any man will perform best when he is relaxed and feeling good about himself. Give him sex often enough and offer it with no strings attached. A man will change, soften, try new things and be more attentive to you if he is feeling satisfied. If you show him what you want and let him feel appreciated and loved, he will try to adapt. He will gradually move toward sweeter, slower actions that include talking intimately, stroking, hugging and kissing before having sex. Please don't try to direct the show through criticism. Men want to know what to do and how to please you, so show him what to do and tell him gently and kindly.

If you are giving to your man, and understanding of his sexual needs, you will go a long way toward keeping him satisfied. If your man doesn't want sex with you, it may be because of changes in his body. As a man ages, his testosterone level drops, which can lessen his desire to have sex. Please help your man take this seriously; treatment is readily available.

A man may also lose sexual desire because of trouble in your relationship. He may feel so alienated and unappreciated that he has given up on sex with you. In my experience, men are happiest when they can have sex frequently, freely and enjoyably with their wives. For a man, sex is usually a very important part of his relationship. If he feels satisfied sexually, he's much more likely to cooperate and give you what you need and want. Sometimes, good sex will bring a man close to you like nothing else will.

Thank you for reading what I have to say to women. I hope it has been helpful. I also hope you find a way to get your mate to read this book and that he finds it helpful as well. We men have so much potential in the area of relationships. I encourage you to value men and to respect their unique contributions to marriage. Men and women need each other, and marriage provides us a terrific opportunity to learn about ourselves and to learn to love another person fully. May your marriage bring you deep self-knowledge and great love.

How Can Marty Friedman Help You?

Marty Friedman is available to speak to your group, organization or association about his insights into men, women and relationships. An accomplished speaker and seminar leader who has presented more than 2,000 speeches or workshops over 25 years, he tailors each presentation to fit his audience's needs.

Keynote speeches or short break-out groups are inspiring, funny and poignant; Marty Friedman paints a picture of 21st-century relationships and marriage, and how men need to change their view of marriage and women need to change their views of men. Longer workshops or seminars delve into the concepts and techniques in this book, and provide participants the opportunity to fundamentally change the path of their intimate relationships.

Men also are invited to work with Marty Friedman in private telephone or in-person discussions. Working one-on-one allows you time to explore your unique situation, assess how you can apply his relationship principles, identify a plan for change, receive constructive feedback, review your progress and develop long-term goals. A few conversations can make a big difference in the quality of your relationship—and your life.

Marty Friedman's straight talk, no-therapy approach reveals to men why they are challenged in marriage—and what to do about it. And his insights into the thinking and behavior of married men help women and men restore the joy to their lives and marriages. Best of all, he "walks the walk": everything he says comes from his own experience and struggles.

To learn more about Marty Friedman, his work and seminar and consulting schedule, call (866) 627-3518 or visit his website at www.meninmarriage.com.

Marty Friedman
Founder, Men in Marriage
"Strong Men, Strong Marriages. It's Not What You Think."

555 Bryant Street, #581
Palo Alto, CA 94301
Toll Free (866) 627-3518
Fax (302) 264-4134
www.meninmarriage.com
marty@meninmarriage.com

www.meninmarriage.com